THE
PERENNIAL
ENCYCLOPEDIA

THE
PERENNIAL
ENCYCLOPEDIA

John Kilmer

Crescent Books
NEW YORK

A FRIEDMAN GROUP BOOK

This 1989 edition published by Crescent Books
distributed by Crown Publishers, Inc.
225 Park Avenue South
New York, New York 10003

ISBN 0-517-67339-8

PERENNIAL ENCYCLOPEDIA
was prepared and produced by
Michael Friedman Publishing Group, Inc.
15 West 26th Street
New York, New York 10010

Written by John Kilmer
Editor: Sharyn Rosart
Art Director: Robert W. Kosturko
Designer: David Shultz
Photography Editor: Christopher Bain
Production Manager: Karen L. Greenberg

Typeset by BPE Graphics
Color separations by Universal Colour Scanning Ltd.
Printed and bound in Hong Kong by Leefung-Asco Printers Ltd.

h g f e d c b a

Dedication
To my old friend HVP Wilson

Acknowledgments
Thanks to the people at Van
Winden Garden Center for their cooperation

CONTENTS

Part I
INTRODUCTION TO PERENNIALS

Perennials are the backbone of any good garden because they supply bright color year after year. However, certain perennials have a short bloom season, others a long season, and some die right after flowering. For simplicity, we say that perennials usually bloom in the year after they have been planted; but if they are planted early in certain climates, many perennials will bloom the same year. Perennials belong to a group of plants called "herbaceous" plants. Annuals and flowering bulbs are also classified as herbacious plants—having *soft* stems. Trees and shrubs belong to a different group collectively known as "woody" plants because they form a durable cell structure called wood.

Select perennials according to their bloom season: one group for spring, one for summer, and one for fall. For color all year, supplement the garden with annuals and bulbs.

Far left: *Coreopsis, lilies, and black-eyed Susan dominate a midsummer garden.* Near left: *Annuals and perennials can be intermingled to heighten the garden's color. A whole new group of perennials comes into bloom as fall approaches* (below).

Perennials are the color workhorse of the garden and can be used to make designs. They add color to landscapes that consist only of trees and shrubs; they are the basis for informal flower, cutting, or cottage gardens; and they are so versatile that they create beauty in the formal landscape, too. The basic perennial border is a time-honored use of flowers in the landscape.

Varieties

Perennials, like all plants, are called by their universally acceptable botanical names. Common names are also used, but are not always reliable; for example, in one area of the country a particular plant is called Black-eyed Susan, but in another area it is known as Rudbeckia Daisy. Most perennials have been hybridized or propagated to create plants that are improved in some way—bigger flowers, longer blooming seasons, or better colors or forms. These hybrids are designated as varieties. Variety names are enclosed in single quotes, for example: *Rudbeckia fulgida* 'Goldsturm.'

Planting Design

THE SIZE AND CONTOUR OF YOUR GARDEN SITE WILL AFFECT YOUR GARDEN DESIGN. IF YOU ARE USING PERENNIALS IN A BED OR DRIFT, PLANT THEM ONLY THIRTY INCHES WIDE SO YOU CAN EASILY TEND THE FLOWERS AT THE BACK. HOWEVER, AN ISLAND BED OR DRIFT EASILY REACHED FROM ALL SIDES CAN BE SIXTY INCHES ACROSS. PLANT TALL FLOWERS SUCH AS DELPHINIUMS AND STOCK IN THE REAR OF THE BED, MEDIUM ONES IN THE MIDDLE, AND SMALL PLANTS UP FRONT. ALWAYS AVOID A STRAIGHT-ROW

Low-growing perennials (below left) *provide a
carpet of color to shrubs in spring. By selecting perennials
that bloom at different times, you can be sure there will
always be plants in flower* (below right).

SOLDIERLIKE GARDEN DESIGN. INSTEAD, PLANT CIRCULAR OR OVAL MASSES (DRIFTS) OF COLOR,

WITH A DOZEN OR MORE GROUPS OVERLAPPING EACH OTHER FOR A DRAMATIC EFFECT.

TO ENSURE THAT YOU HAVE A WELL-PLANNED

PERENNIAL GARDEN, FIRST DRAW SEVERAL ROUGH SKETCHES OF THE SITE. NOTE ON THE

SKETCHES THE LOCATIONS OF PATHS AND WALKS, AND WHERE SHRUBS, TREES, AND HEDGES NOW

STAND. AFTER THIS STEP IT WILL BE EASY TO SELECT THE APPROPRIATE PERENNIALS FOR THE SITE.

YOU WILL WANT TO ESTABLISH A CERTAIN CHARACTER: AN INFORMAL COTTAGE LOOK, WHERE

EVERYTHING IS SIMPLY MIXED TOGETHER, OR A FORMAL LOOK. THE FORMAL GARDEN WILL BE

DIFFICULT TO CREATE WITH MATURE TREES AND SHRUBS BECAUSE IT MUST BE SYMMETRICAL—

TWO OF THIS, THREE OF THAT, AND SO ON, WITH ONE SIDE USUALLY MIRRORING THE OTHER. IF

THE SITE IS FLAT AND LACKING MANY ESTABLISHED TREES OR SHRUBS, EITHER THE FORMAL OR

INFORMAL PLAN IS FINE.

TO CREATE AN INFORMAL COTTAGE GARDEN, PLAN FOR CURVES OR DRIFTS OF FLOWERS WITH

WIDE ARCS MATCHING THE GENERAL FLOW OF THE SITE. WHETHER THE DESIGN IS FORMAL OR

INFORMAL, PLANT PERENNIALS IN BORDERS OR DRIFTS, OR BOTH IF YOU HAVE THE SPACE.

A PERENNIAL BORDER IS A FLOW OF COLOR THAT DEFINES A LAWN OR WALKWAY. A DRIFT IS A MASS OF FLOWERS IN CURVING BEDS OR ARCS. NOTE THAT DRIFTS OF FLOWERS USUALLY NEED AMPLE SPACE. IF YOU PLACE JUST ONE BED IN A GARDEN, IT WILL LOOK LIKE AN UNATTRACTIVE PUNCTUATION MARK. YOU NEED AT LEAST THREE OR FOUR BEDS TO CREATE A RICH, FLOWERY GARDEN.

BEDS OF FLOWERS ARE ACCESSIBLE AND VISIBLE FROM ALL SIDES. BORDERS, ON THE OTHER HAND, ARE MORE LINEAR AND ALLOW MORE OPEN SPACE IN THE GARDEN. THE BORDER GARDEN

The best visual effect is achieved when perennials are planted in large clumps (below).

DEPENDS ON THE OPEN SPACE IT ACCENTS. THERE SHOULD BE AN APPROPRIATE BALANCE BETWEEN THE BORDERS AND THE REST OF THE SITE. BORDERS ARE ALSO GOOD FOR SOFTENING SEVERE LINES OF BUILDINGS, FENCES, AND WALKWAYS.

TO START YOUR GARDEN, DECIDE WHETHER IT IS GOING TO BE ALL PERENNIAL OR A MIXED BED, AND WITH A SEASONAL ACCENT OR A CONTINUOUS FLOW OF COLOR FOR EACH SEASON. CONSIDER HEIGHT, BLOOMING TIME, AND COLOR. SPACING IS IMPORTANT, TOO: MOST PERENNI- ALS CAN BE PLANTED ABOUT TWELVE INCHES APART.

Planting and General Care

Iғ ʏᴏᴜ ᴡᴀɴᴛ ᴛᴏ ɢʀᴏᴡ ɢᴏᴏᴅ ᴘᴇʀᴇɴɴɪᴀʟs (ᴏʀ ᴀɴʏ ᴘʟᴀɴᴛs), ʏᴏᴜ ᴍᴜsᴛ ᴘʀᴇᴘᴀʀᴇ ᴛʜᴇ sᴏɪʟ ʙʏ ᴅɪɢɢɪɴɢ ᴏᴜᴛ ᴀʙᴏᴜᴛ ᴛᴡᴇɴᴛʏ ɪɴᴄʜᴇs ᴀɴᴅ ʀᴇᴄᴏɴᴅɪᴛɪᴏɴɪɴɢ ɪᴛ. Mᴏsᴛ sᴏɪʟs ᴍᴜsᴛ ʙᴇ ʀᴇᴄᴏɴᴅɪᴛɪᴏɴᴇᴅ ɪɴ ᴏʀᴅᴇʀ ᴛᴏ ɢʀᴏᴡ ᴘᴇʀᴇɴɴɪᴀʟs sᴜᴄᴄᴇssғᴜʟʟʏ. Aᴅᴅ ᴀɴ ᴏʀɢᴀɴɪᴄ ғᴇʀᴛɪʟɪᴢᴇʀ sᴜᴄʜ ᴀs ᴄᴏᴛᴛᴏɴsᴇᴇᴅ ᴍᴇᴀʟ, ᴄʜɪᴄᴋᴇɴ ᴍᴀɴᴜʀᴇ, ᴏʀ ᴄᴏᴍᴘᴏsᴛ—ᴀʟʟ sᴏʟᴅ ɪɴ ᴛɪᴅʏ sᴀᴄᴋs ᴀᴛ ɴᴜʀsᴇʀɪᴇs. Wᴏʀᴋ ᴛʜᴇ ᴍᴀᴛᴇʀɪᴀʟ ɪɴᴛᴏ ᴛʜᴇ ɢʀᴏᴜɴᴅ ᴛʜᴏʀᴏᴜɢʜʟʏ; ɪғ ᴘᴏssɪʙʟᴇ, ᴀᴅᴅ ɴᴇᴡ ᴛᴏᴘsᴏɪʟ. Bᴇ sᴜʀᴇ ᴛʜᴇ sᴏɪʟ ɪs ᴘᴏʀᴏᴜs sᴏ ᴛʜᴀᴛ ᴡᴀᴛᴇʀ ᴀɴᴅ ᴀɪʀ ᴄᴀɴ ʀᴜɴ ᴛʜʀᴏᴜɢʜ ɪᴛ ᴇᴀsɪʟʏ.

At planting time, dig large holes to accommodate the root balls of the perennials, and be sure to tuck the soil firmly around the collars of the plants. Pat down the soil with your palms. Plants can be put into the ground in fall or spring. It is best to plant early-blooming varieties in the fall, late bloomers in the spring.

Perennials need good drainage to thrive; make sure the soil is friable (easily crumbled) and drains well. Be sure plants are in a reasonably sunny location. Most perennials need sun or light shade; few grow in dark, shady places.

Watering is vital to all plants, especially perennials, to provide needed moisture for abundant bloom. Your geographic location will determine how much water your plants will need. In areas with frequent rainfall, only occasional watering is necessary, but in dry areas, plants must be watered two or three times a week. And watering does not mean sprinkling. It takes water four hours to penetrate twenty-four-inch soil, so a few minutes of watering with a hand-held hose does little good. Srinklers invariably waste more water than they furnish to roots. A drip-watering system is the answer. This inexpensive system regularly and constantly waters where it is needed—at the roots—so plants grow rapidly.

Perennials do not need a massive feeding program. They do quite well with very little food, perhaps a general 10-10-5 fertilizer twice a year. More frequent feeding is necessary only if your soil is depleted of nutrients, in which case you should feed plants more often.

Below: *Although they are low-maintenance plants, daylilies, like all perennials, have certain requirements for soil, water, and nutrition.*

Selecting Colors

ONCE YOU HAVE DESIGNED YOUR GARDEN, YOU MUST CHOOSE COLORS. DO YOU WANT A ONE-COLOR SCHEME, OR DO YOU PREFER A CHANGING GARDEN, WITH DIFFERENT COLORS FROM SEASON TO SEASON? DO YOU WANT TALL PLANTS OR SHORT ONES? WHAT ABOUT THE WAY COLORS LOOK TOGETHER? BLUE FLOWERS NEXT TO YELLOW ONES JOLT THE EYE; RED MIXED WITH BLUE IS NOT VERY ATTRACTIVE EITHER. STRIVE FOR

Large blocks of color help the eye to move from one section of the garden to another (below). Pink and blue harmonize well together (opposite) and their combination is an example of split-complementary harmony.

GRADATIONS OF COLOR IN YOUR PERENNIAL GARDEN: USE RED, RED-ORANGE, AND YELLOW-ORANGE IN A GROUPING. THE PSYCHOLOGY OF COLOR IN THE GARDEN DESERVES A BOOK OF ITS OWN, SO HERE I WILL ONLY RECOMMEND THAT YOU MIX AND MATCH COLORS CAREFULLY. USE MONOCHROMATIC COLOR SCHEMES OR GRADATIONS OF COLOR WHEN SELECTING PLANT COLORS.

The Cutting Garden

THE CUTTING GARDEN IS JUSTIFIABLY A FAVORITE OF MANY GARDENERS BECAUSE THERE IS NOTHING AS SATISFYING TO THE SOUL AS GOING INTO THE GARDEN AND CUTTING YOUR OWN FLOWERS. THIS TYPE OF GARDEN SHOULD BE PLANNED IN A RECTANGULAR SITE, LIKE A VEGETABLE GARDEN. IN THE NINETEENTH CENTURY, THE CUTTING GARDEN WAS A STAPLE OF ALL LANDSCAPES AND GENERALLY WAS LOCATED NEAR THE KITCHEN FOR EASY ACCESS. TODAY, THE CUTTING GARDEN IS USED ALMOST ANY PLACE IN THE YARD, BUT USUALLY IT IS NOT A PART OF THE OVERALL PLANTING DESIGN.

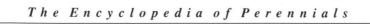

Grooming and Maintenance

Single-stalked perennials such as gladi-
oli, hollyhocks, and delphiniums will require staking, as will floppy-stemmed plants
like coreopsis. You can buy tall, slender bamboo stakes at nurseries. Place the
bamboo stakes an inch or more from the plants; plunge the stakes into the ground
so they are stable; then tie the stakes to the plants with "tie-ems" or string.

Notes:

THE PLANTS LISTED AS PARTNERS FOR A SPE-
CIFIC PLANT ARE ONLY SUGGESTED COMPANIONS. YOUR COLOR PREFERENCES MAY DIFFER FROM
MINE AND, IF THEY DO, YOUR COMBINATIONS WILL DIFFER FROM THOSE I HAVE SUGGESTED. AS
WELL, LISTS OF CULTIVARS, IF ANY, ARE NOT EXHAUSTIVE, BUT SIMPLY GIVE AN IDEA OF WHAT IS
AVAILABLE. IN SOME PARTS OF THE COUNTRY, PERENNIALS MAY BE GROWN AS ANNUALS; AND SOME
ANNUALS MAY BE CONSIDERED BIENNIAL, BLOOMING A SECOND YEAR.

Below: *Botanically, bearded iris is* Iris germanica. Iris
is the genus; germanica *is the species. With any genus there may
be few to many species.* Opposite: *Oriental poppy is an extremely
hardy perennial, surviving winters as cold as -40° F.*

Botanical names of plants frequently differ around the world, or plant names may be changed by taxonomists as they gain new knowledge of plants and their distribution. I have generally tried to use the names as listed in most mail-order suppliers' catalogs. Names were also checked with *Hortus III*.

The climate zone map is most helpful in determining what can grow where, but within each zone there are microclimates where temperatures may be ten to fifteen degrees above or below the average zone temperature stated.

Metric measurement equivalents are approximate throughout this book.

I have not included specific planting times for plants, because they vary throughout North America. Generally, it is safe to plant when plants are available in nurseries—in early spring, spring, or late spring.

Part II
THE PLANTS

Acanthus mollis

FAMILY–ACANTHACEAE
COMMON NAME–BEAR'S BREECH

Origin Italy
Leaves Long and green, deeply lobed on stalks
Flowers Mauve, lilac, in bracts on tall stems
Habit Erect to 4 ft (1.2m)
Season of Bloom Summer
Culture Partial shade; will grow in almost any soil
Propagation Division in spring; plant up to 30 in (75cm) apart
Utilization Effective background plant; good against fences and walls
Cultivars 'Latifolius'
Hardiness Zone 5
Partners Ajuga, coreopsis, phlox

Acanthus spinosa

FAMILY–ACANTHACEAE
COMMON NAME–SPINY BEAR'S
BREECH

Origin Europe
Leaves Dark green, deeply divided with spiny points
Flowers Mauve, hidden in bracts on tall spikes
Habit Erect but somewhat arching
Season of Bloom Summer
Culture Shade; grows in almost any soil
Propagation Division in spring; plant up to 30 in (75cm) apart
Utilization Effective background plant; good against fences, walls, or to define a planting bed
Hardiness Zone 5
Partners Ajuga, coreopsis, phlox

Achillea filipendula

FAMILY–COMPOSITAE
COMMON NAME–FERNLEAFED
YARROW

Origin Europe
Leaves Feathery green, spicy odor, alternate
Flowers Flat heads of yellow flowers, raceme 12 ft (4m) across
Habit Erect to 4 ft (1.2m)
Season of Bloom Summer
Culture Sun or partial sun; will tolerate drought
Propagation Division
Utilization Good background or bedding plants; specimen plant; nice foliage effect
Cultivars 'Cornation Gold,' 'Gold Plate,' 'Moonshine,' 'Parker's Variety'
Hardiness Zone 3
Partners Delphinium, gomphrena, salvia

Achillea millefolium
'Rosea'

FAMILY–COMPOSITAE
COMMON NAME–PINK-FLOWERED
YARROW

Origin Hybrid
Leaves Mats of bright green, feathery, dissected leaves
Flowers Flat heads of pale pink flowers, .25 in (6mm) across in flat corymbs 3 in (8cm) across
Habit Erect to 3 ft (1m)
Season of Bloom Summer
Culture Sun; will tolerate drought
Propagation Division in spring or autumn; plant up to 12 in (30cm) apart
Utilization Graceful background plant for perennial borders
Hardiness Zone 2
Partners Delphinium, gomphrena, salvia

Achillea ptarmica

FAMILY–COMPOSITAE
COMMON NAME–SNEEZEWEED

Origin Europe
Leaves Green, feathery, rangy, to 4 in (10cm) long
Flowers White heads of .5 in (1.2cm) flowers in loose clusters
Habit May need staking; grows to 2 ft (.6m)
Season of Bloom Summer
Culture Sun; moist soil

Propagation Division in spring or autumn; plant up to 16 in (40cm) apart
Utilization Attractive cut flowers; good as a background plant; effective mass of color
Cultivars 'Angel's Breath,' 'The Pearl'
Hardiness Zone 2
Partners Chrysanthemum, gomphrena

Achillea schwellenberg

FAMILY–COMPOSITAE
COMMON NAME–NONE

Origin Asia, Europe
Leaves Silver-gray leaves, toothed
Flowers Small yellow flowerheads in abundance
Habit Erect to 36 in (1m)
Season of Bloom Summer
Culture Partial sun; average soil

Propagation Division in spring; plant up to 16 in (40cm) apart
Utilization Good in borders
Cultivars 'Moonshine'
Hardiness Zone 4
Partners Coreopsis, helenium, heliopsis

Adenophora confusa

FAMILY–CAMPANULACEAE
COMMON NAME–BELLFLOWER

Origin Asia
Leaves Alternate, lanceolate, arched
Flowers Blue bell-shaped flowers on tall spines, spaced alternately
Habit Erect to 3 ft (1m)
Season of Bloom Summer
Culture Sun; well-drained soil
Propagation Division in spring
Utilization Good background bedding plant; dramatic color accent
Hardiness Zone 4
Partners Arabis, cerastium

Ajuga reptans

FAMILY–LABIATA
COMMON NAME–BUGLEWEED

Origin Europe
Leaves 2- to 4-in shiny green leaves that form a rosette 6 in high
Flowers Red or purple; .25 in
Habit Spreading, invasive
Season of Bloom Spring
Culture Will grow well in shade; moist, porous soil
Propagation Runners; plant up to 8 in (20cm) apart
Utilization Outstanding for ground cover; good for edging or mass planting
Cultivars 'Alba,' 'Burgundy Glow'
Hardiness Zone 4
Partners Chrysanthemum, lily

Allium schoenoprasum

FAMILY–ALLIACEAE
COMMON NAME–CHIVES

Origin Northern Hemisphere
Leaves Bright green, similar to daffodil
leaves
Flowers Tight heads of rosy lilac flowers
Habit Erect to 2 ft (60cm)
Season of Bloom Summer
Culture Sun; will grow in poor soil
Propagation Division; plant up to 10 in
(25cm) apart
Utilization Effective background plant;
good in an herb garden; attractive
cut flowers
Cultivars 'Sibericum'
Hardiness Zone 3
Partners Ajuga, dictamus, gypsophila

Alstroemaria pulchella
(ligtu)

FAMILY–AMARYLLIDACEAE
COMMON NAME–PERUVIAN LILY

Origin Brazil
Leaves Gray-green, leggy, twisted at
base
Flowers Rich red-brown, lilylike, in
clusters
Habit Sprawling, grows in clumps
Season of Bloom Summer or fall

Culture Sun; moist soil
Propagation Division, seed; plant up to
12 in (30cm) apart
Utilization Good cut flowers; colorful
bedding plant when used in mass
Hardiness Zone 4
Partners Arabis, campanula, phlox

Anchusa myosotidiflora

FAMILY–BORAGINACEAE
COMMON NAME–ALKANET

Origin Europe
Leaves Dense, cordate, alternate
Flowers Small blue flowers in clusters
Habit Dense clump growth to 18 in
(45cm)
Season of Bloom Summer
Culture Partial shade; well-drained soil

Propagation Division; plant up to 12 in
(30cm) apart
Utilization Good bedding plant; use in
rock gardens
Cultivars 'Blue Angel'
Hardiness Zone 4
Partners Fern, geranium, hosta

Anemone japonica

FAMILY–RANUNCULACEAE
COMMON NAME–WINDFLOWER

Origin China
Leaves Divided or lobed, mostly basal
Flowers Soft rose-pink flowers on
branching stems
Habit Wiry stems; clump growth to 2 to
3 ft (60cm to 1m)
Season of Bloom Late summer or fall
Culture Sun; prefers poor soil

Propagation Root cuttings, division;
plant up to 18 in (45cm) apart
Utilization Good specimen plants; effec-
tive in perennial borders
Cultivars 'Honore Jobert,' 'September
Charm,' 'Max Vogel,' 'Prince Henry'
Hardiness Zone 5
Partners Ajuga, chrysanthemum

Anigozanthos flavidus

FAMILY–HAEMODORACEAE
COMMON NAME–KANGAROO PAW

Origin Australia
Leaves Swordlike, coarse, evergreen
Flowers Upward-facing, rusty-red, trumpet-shaped flowers have yellow tips resembling a small claw, formed in clusters that make conspicuous flower spikes produced over a period of several months
Habit Clump-forming, tall, growing to 5 ft (1.5m) high
Season of Bloom Early to late summer
Culture Will tolerate poor soil and drought
Propagation By seed and division
Utilization For containers and sparingly in mixed borders
Hardiness Zone 9
Partners Agapanthus, daylily, iris

Aquilegia alpina

FAMILY–RANUNCULACEAE
COMMON NAME–COLUMBINE

Origin Switzerland
Leaves Smooth, gray or gray-green, compound
Flowers Pale blue with spurs, resemble shooting stars
Habit Graceful form, grows 1 to 3 ft (30cm to 1m)
Season of Bloom Spring
Culture Sun; moist soil
Propagation Seed; plant up to 12 in (30cm) apart
Utilization Good for perennial borders; effective color
Cultivars 'Red Star'
Hardiness Zone 3
Partners Arabis, iris

Arabis albida
(caucasica)

FAMILY–CRUCIFERAE
COMMON NAME–WHITE
ROCKCRESS

Origin European Alps
Leaves Gray-felted, basal
Flowers White, .5 in (1.2cm) across in loose clusters
Habit Low and spreading, grows to 1 ft (30cm)
Season of Bloom Spring
Culture Sun; porous soil

Propagation Division; plant up to 10 in (25cm) apart
Utilization Good in rock gardens or front of borders; edging
Cultivars 'Flore Pleno'
Hardiness Zone 3
Partners Arabis, phlox

Armeria maritima

FAMILY–PLUMBAGINACEAE
COMMON NAME–SEA PINK;
THRIFT

Origin Europe
Leaves Dense grassy leaves in rosettes
Flowers Pink, round, on tall stems
Habit Can form a mat, grows to 2 ft (60cm)
Season of Bloom Spring
Culture Sun; prefers sandy soil

Propagation Division; plant up to 10 in (25cm) apart
Utilization As a low ground cover; great for borders
Cultivars 'Alba,' 'Corsica'
Hardiness Zone 3
Partners Aster, phlox

Artemisia schmidtiana

FAMILY–COMPOSITAE
COMMON NAME–MUGWORT;
SILVER MOUND

Origin Japan
Leaves Gray-green or silver, beautiful foliage
Flowers Very small, white or yellow
Habit Grows into large clumps to 2 ft (60cm) across
Season of Bloom Summer
Culture Will grow in poor soil, but will not tolerate soggy soil

Propagation Division; plant up to 20 in (50cm) apart
Utilization Good edging plant; effective for spot accent; or grow for foliage effect
Cultivars 'Nana,' 'Silver Mound'
Hardiness Zone 3
Partners Aster, gazania, helianthus, phlox

Aster X frikartii

FAMILY–COMPOSITAE
COMMON NAME–HARDY ASTER

Origin North America
Leaves Dense, alternate
Flowers Lavender-blue, daisylike on tall stems
Habit To 20 in (50cm) in clumps
Season of Bloom Summer, fall
Culture Full sun; fertile, well-drained soil

Propagation Division in spring; plant up to 18 in (45cm) apart
Utilization Use in borders or beds
Cultivars 'Wonder of Staffa,' 'Pink Lady'
Hardiness Zone 5
Partners Acanthus, delphinium, gypsophila

Aster novae-angliae

FAMILY–COMPOSITAE
COMMON NAME–MICHAELMAS
DAISY; NEW ENGLAND ASTER

Origin North America
Leaves Narrow, lanceolate, dense
Flowers Mauve or purple, in crowded
    clusters
Habit Erect to 3 to 4 ft (1 to 1.2m)
Season of Bloom Summer, fall
Culture Sun or shade; will tolerate poor
    soil

Propagation Division; plant up to 16 in
    (40cm) apart
Utilization Good specimen plant; fine
    for background
Cultivars 'Barr's Pink,' 'Harrington's
    Bride,' 'Survivor'
Hardiness Zone 4
Partners Chrysanthemum, hemerocallis

*One of the plants that best says "fall" is the aster (below),
which can be combined with mums for a more varied garden.*

Plumes of astilbe (below) *bring a soft grace to the early summer garden.*

Astilbe X arendsii

FAMILY–SAXIFRIGACEAE
COMMON NAME–NONE

Origin Hybrid
Leaves Ferny foliage, dark or red-tinted, simple or component
Flowers Pink, small, grow in clusters
Habit Generally erect, grows to 3 ft (1m)
Season of Bloom Summer, fall
Culture Dislikes dry or soggy soil; should be shaded from direct sun
Propagation Division; plant up to 30 in (75cm) apart
Utilization Handsome against rock walls or brick structures
Cultivars 'Deutschland,' 'Fanal,' 'Federsee,' 'Peach Blossom'
Hardiness Zone 4
Partners Asarum, fern, helianthus, hemerocallis

Aubretia deltoidea

FAMILY–CRUCIFERAE
COMMON NAME–ROCKCRESS

Origin Europe
Leaves Obovate, crowded
Flowers Lilac or pink, in short terminal clusters
Habit Spreading, bushy, to 10 in (25cm)
Season of Bloom Spring, summer
Culture Partial shade; well-drained soil
Propagation Division; plant up to 10 in (25cm) apart
Utilization Good in rock gardens; for borders or edging
Cultivars 'Giant Superbissima'
Hardiness Zone 5
Partners Cerastium, cosmos

Aurinia saxatilis

FAMILY–CRUCIFERAE
COMMON NAME–YELLOW
ALYSSUM, BASKET-OF-GOLD

Origin Southern and Central Europe
Leaves Grey-green, lanceolate
Flowers Golden yellow or pale yellow, four-petalled, grouped in dense clusters
Habit Mound-shaped, spreading, 9-12 in (22-30cm) high
Season of Bloom Early spring
Culture Full sun; will tolerate poor soil, providing drainage is good
Propagation Seeds and by cuttings
Utilization Good in rock gardens and dry walls; also for edging beds and borders
Hardiness Zone 4
Partners Spring bulbs, candytuft, columbine, forget-me-not

*Ground-hugging plants like baboonflower are
effective when grown naturally between rocks* (below).

Baptisia australis

FAMILY–LEGUMINOSAE
COMMON NAME–FALSE INDIGO

Origin United States
Leaves Compound, blue-green
Flowers Blue, 1 in (2.5cm) across in terminal racemes
Habit Tall spikes of flowers to 4 ft (1.2m)
Season of Bloom Summer
Culture Sun; well-drained soil
Propagation Division, seed; plant up to 20 in (50cm) apart
Utilization Good accent plant for perennial border
Hardiness Zone 3
Partners Aquilegia, hemerocallis, iberis, primula

Begonia evansiana

FAMILY–BEGONIACEAE
COMMON NAME–HARDY BEGONIA

Origin China, Japan
Leaves Olive-green, ovate, purple underneath
Flowers Bright pink, 1 in (2.5cm) across
Habit Sprawling to 24 in (30cm)
Season of Bloom Summer
Culture Partial shade; evenly moist soil
Propagation Division in spring
Utilization Good background plant; provides mass in garden
Hardiness Zone 4
Partners Ageratum, phlox

Bergenia cordifolia

FAMILY–SAXIFRAGACEAE
COMMON NAME–HEART-LEAVED
BERGENIA

Origin Siberia
Leaves Rounded, bullate, crinkled at
  edges
Flowers Mauve-pink or white flowers in
  large heads
Habit Low growing to about 2 ft (60cm)
Season of Bloom Summer, spring
Culture Shade or sun; any soil

Propagation Division; plant up to 24 in
  (60cm) apart
Utilization Excellent ground cover;
  effective foliage plant
Cultivars 'Alba,' 'Perfecta,' 'Purpurea'
Hardiness Zone 2
Partners Best used alone as ground
  cover

Campanula glomerata

FAMILY–CAMPANULACEAE
COMMON NAME–BELLFLOWER

Origin Europe, Asia
Leaves Ovate, bright green, attractive,
  basal
Flowers Purple bell-shaped flowers, al-
  ternate on short stems
Habit Tall, erect to 2 ft (60cm)
Season of Bloom Summer
Culture Shade; tolerates wet soil

Propagation Division; plant up to 24 in
  (60cm) apart
Utilization Invaluable for grouping
  with most plants
Cultivars 'Alba,' 'Joan Elliott,' 'Su-
  perba'
Hardiness Zone 3
Partners Anemone, primula, shrub rose

Campanula persicifolia
'White Star'

FAMILY–CAMPANULACEAE
COMMON NAME–PEACH-LEAVED
BELLFLOWER

Origin Europe, Asia
Leaves Evergreen, basal rosettes of narrow leaves
Flowers Lilac-blue on wiry stems
Habit Erect to 3 ft (1m)
Season of Bloom Summer
Culture Shade or sun; well-drained soil
Propagation Seed; plant up to 24 in (60cm) apart
Utilization Good accent for borders or edging; good cut flower
Hardiness Zone 3
Partners Anemone, monarda, old rose

Catananche caerulea

FAMILY–COMPOSITAE
COMMON NAME–CUPID'S DART

Origin Europe
Leaves Narrow gray-green, mostly basal
Flowers Blue, 2 in (5cm) across on wiry stems
Habit Clump grown; erect stems to 18 in (45cm)
Season of Bloom Summer
Culture Full sun; good drainage
Propagation Root cuttings, seed; plant up to 12 in (30cm) apart
Utilization Good for drying for everlasting bouquets
Hardiness Zone 4
Partners Achillea, chrysanthemum, gypsophila, phlox

Centaurea cineraria

FAMILY–COMPOSITAE
COMMON NAME–DUSTY MILLER

Origin Mediterranean region
Leaves Tall, covered with white hairs, alternate
Flowers Yellow in tufts
Habit Erect to 3 ft (1m)
Season of Bloom Summer
Culture Sun; well-drained soil

Propagation By prestarted plants; plant up to 24 in (60cm) apart
Utilization Border or edge plant, excellent as foliage accent
Hardiness Zone 4
Partners Chrysanthemum, platycodon

Centaurea macrocephala

FAMILY–COMPOSITAE
COMMON NAME–YELLOW
THISTLE

Origin Caucasus Mountains, Europe
Leaves Lanceolate, floppy, coarse, dark green
Flowers Golden yellow, thistlelike, 3 to 4 in (7.5-10cm) across, held erect by papery, brown bracts
Habit Clump-forming, erect, 3 to 4 ft (1-1.2m) high
Season of Bloom Early summer
Culture Full sun, moist, loam soil
Propagation By division and by seed
Utilization Good for cutting and as a dried flower, background highlight for mixed borders
Hardiness Zone 3
Partners Bearded iris, oriental poppy, peony

Centaurea montana

FAMILY–COMPOSITAE
COMMON NAME–CORNFLOWER

Origin Europe
Leaves Gray-green, crinkled at edges, leggy, diverse forms
Flowers Blue, spidery flowers, 3 in (7.5cm) across
Habit Sprawling, grows to 3 ft (1m)
Season of Bloom Summer
Culture Sun; average soil, neither too dry nor too moist
Propagation Division; plant up to 24 in (60cm) apart
Utilization Good in perennial drifts, as edging, or in rock gardens
Hardiness Zone 2
Partners Chrysanthemum, platycodon

Centranthus (Valerian) ruber

FAMILY–VALERIANACEAE
COMMON NAME–RED VALERIAN

Origin Mediterranean
Leaves Opposite, generally toothed
Flowers Pink or white
Habit Bushy to 36 in (1m)
Season of Bloom Summer
Culture Sun; well-drained soil
Propagation Cuttings; seed in spring; plant up to 16 in (40cm) apart
Utilization Good background or bedding plant
Hardiness Zone 5
Partners Catanche, centaurea, chrysanthemum

Cerastium tomentosum

FAMILY–CARYOPHYLLACEAE
COMMON NAME–
SNOW-IN-SUMMER

Origin Europe
Leaves Opposite, hairy, dense
Flowers Masses of small white flowers
   in feathery clusters
Habit Prostrate to 6 in (15cm)
Season of Bloom Summer
Culture Sun; well-drained soil
Propagation Division; plant up to 14 in
   (35cm) apart
Utilization Good for borders, effective
   as edging
Hardiness Zone 4
Partners Coreopsis, geranium, phlox,
   veronica

Chrysanthemum coronarium

FAMILY–COMPOSITAE
COMMON NAME–CROWN DAISY

Origin Europe
Leaves Pinnate, sharply grooved seg-
   ments
Flowers Yellow daisylike flowers in pro-
   fusion
Habit Mounds of color; grows to about
   2 ft (60cm)
Season of Bloom Summer
Culture Partial shade; well-drained soil
Propagation Scatter seed in garden as
   soon as earth is friable; thin and
   transplant; plant up to 16 in (40cm)
   apart
Utilization Masses of color in flower
   bed
Hardiness Zone 5
Partners Cosmos, mirabilis, zinnia

Chrysanthemum X morifolium

FAMILY–COMPOSITAE
COMMON NAME–
CHRYSANTHEMUM

Origin Hybrid
Leaves Alternate, divided, gray, hairy
Flowers In heads, most colors except blue
Habit Dense, bushy, grows to 18 ft (6m)
Season of Bloom Fall
Culture Sun; well-drained soil
Propagation Division
Utilization Use in drifts and flower beds
Cultivars 'Petit Point Mix,' many others
Hardiness Zone 5
Partners Cosmos, phlox, rudbeckia

Chrysanthemum nipponicum

FAMILY–COMPOSITAE
COMMON NAME–NIPPON DAISY

Origin Japan
Leaves Gray-green, fernlike, divided
Flowers White, 2 to 3 in (5 to 7.5cm) across on branching stems
Habit Bushy; grows to 2 ft (60cm)
Season of Bloom Fall
Culture Partial shade; good drainage; even, moist soil
Propagation Division; plant up to 20 in (50cm) apart
Utilization Good in drifts or against fences; attractive cut flowers
Hardiness Zone 5
Partners Helianthus, monarda

Chrysanthemum parthenium

FAMILY–COMPOSITAE
COMMON NAME–FEVERFEW

Origin Europe
Leaves Segmented, dense
Flowers Button-head, white flowers
Habit Forms clumps to 1 ft (30cm)
Season of Bloom Summer
Culture Sun; well-drained soil
Propagation Scatter seed as soon as earth is friable; plant up to 12 in (30cm) apart
Utilization In flower beds where mass of color is needed
Hardiness Zone 5
Partners Helianthus, monarda

Chrysogonum virginiana

FAMILY–COMPOSITAE
COMMON NAME–GOLDEN STAR

Origin United States
Leaves Scalloped, large, bluntly toothed
Flowers Yellow, sparse
Habit Forms clumps to about 10 in (25cm)
Season of Bloom Summer
Culture Sun or light shade; even moisture
Propagation Division; plant up to 12 in (30cm) apart
Utilization Low border plant, good spot color
Hardiness Zone 5
Partners Fern, phlox divaricata

Below: *A well-designed perennial garden uses a
combination of spiked, mounded, and low-growing plants.*

Clematis recta

FAMILY–RANUNCULACEAE
COMMON NAME–GROUND
CLEMATIS

Origin Southern Europe
Leaves Dark green, lanceolate
Flowers White, fragrant, individually
1 in (2.5cm) across, clustered at the
top of the tall-growing plants
Habit Erect, clump-forming
Season of Bloom Early summer
Culture Moist, fertile, loam soil in full
sun
Propagation By seed and by division
Utilization Tall background highlight in
mixed borders
Hardiness Zone 5
Partners Dictamnus, filipendulina

Coreopsis grandiflora
'Sunray'

FAMILY–COMPOSITAE
COMMON NAME–NONE

Origin Hybrid
Leaves Long, slender, lobed or dissected
Flowers Yellow, 3 in (7.5cm) across on
wiry stems
Habit Somewhat sprawling, to 3 ft (1m)
Season of Bloom Summer
Culture Sun; adapts to most soils
Propagation Division; plant up to 20 in
(50cm) apart
Utilization Good accent in any garden,
fine cut flower
Cultivars 'Badengold,' 'Goldfink,' 'May-
field Giant'
Hardiness Zone 5
Partners Delphinium, hemerocallis,
veronica

Coreopsis verticillata

FAMILY–COMPOSITAE
COMMON NAME–THREADLEAF
COREOPSIS

Origin United States
Leaves Fine-haired, lobed or dissected
Flowers Yellow, 2 in (5cm) across on tall stems
Habit Dense, upright bushy to 2 ft (60cm)
Season of Bloom Summer or fall
Culture Sun; easily grown in almost any soil
Propagation Division; plant up to 18 in (45cm) apart
Utilization Makes a show by itself, good cut flower
Cultivars 'Moonbeam,' 'Sunray,' 'Zagreb'
Hardiness Zone 5
Partners Delphinium, hemerocallis, veronica

Crocosmia X crocosmiflora (montebretia)

FAMILY–IRIDACEAE
COMMON NAME–MONTEBRETIA

Origin Hybrid
Leaves Green, arching, grassy
Flowers Orange-red on tall, spirelike stems
Habit Erect to 4 ft (1.2m)
Season of Bloom Summer
Culture Sun or partial shade; well-drained soil
Propagation Division; plant up to 12 in (30cm) apart
Utilization Good vertical accent in borders or drifts
Hardiness Zone 5
Partners Ceanothos, hemerocallis

*The mid- to late summer perennial garden is
enhanced with the brilliant flowers of montbretia* (below).

Crocosmia (montbretia) masonorum

FAMILY–IRIDACEAE
COMMON NAME–MONTEBRETIA

Origin South Africa
Leaves Broad, palmate
Flowers Red, on tall spirelike stems
Habit Erect to 5 ft (1.6m)
Season of Bloom Summer
Culture Sun or partial shade; will tolerate poor soil
Propagation Division; plant up to 12 in (30cm) apart
Utilization Good vertical accent in drifts or borders
Hardiness Zone 5
Partners Achillea, hemerocallis, phlox

Cyclamen repandum

FAMILY–PRIMULCEAE
COMMON NAME–PERSIAN VIOLET

Origin Mediterranean
Leaves Rounded, serrated, glossy blue-green with silvery zone
Flowers Nodding, white, pink, and rosy-red flowers with petals swept back and upwards, about 1-½ in (3cm) long on slender stems
Habit Rosette-forming, colony-forming, ground-hugging
Season of Bloom Spring
Culture Partial shade; prefers cool, woodsy well-drained soil with high organic content, especially leaf mold
Propagation Forms bulbous corms that can be divided
Utilization Good in woodland gardens or as edging for paths
Hardiness Zone 5
Partners Bluebell, Jacob's ladder, primroses, violet

Delphinium x Belladonna

FAMILY–RANUNCULACEAE
COMMON NAME–BELLADONNA
DELPHINIUM

Origin Hybrids of species native to China and Northern Europe
Leaves Maplelike, indented, serrated
Flowers Mostly blue and white
Habit Erect, clump-forming
Season of Bloom Early summer
Culture Full sun; prefers cool, moist, loam soil
Propagation By seed, start in late summer to flower the following year
Utilization Massed as highlights in mixed borders; good for cutting
Hardiness Zone 4
Partners Eryngium, Iceland poppies, verbascum

Delphinium 'Pacific Hybrids'

FAMILY–RANUNCULACEAE
COMMON NAME–DELPHINIUM

Origin Hybrid
Leaves Alternate, lobed
Flowers Columns of blue, violet, and white flowers
Habit Elegant, erect to 5 ft (1.6m)
Season of Bloom Summer
Culture Partial sun; moist soil

Propagation Seed; plant up to 26 in (65cm) apart
Utilization Superior background plant; attractive massed for a special display
Hardiness Zone 3
Partners Phlox, campanula, trollius

Dianthus X alwoodii

FAMILY–CARYOPHYLLACEAE
COMMON NAME–PINK
CARNATIONS

Origin Hybrid
Leaves Blue-green, lanceolate, narrow, opposite
Flowers Pink shades, petals usually fringed
Habit Sprawling hammocks
Season of Bloom Summer
Culture Partial shade; sandy, well-drained soil
Propagation Tip cuttings; plant up to 16 in (40cm) apart
Utilization Attractive in any area of garden; as edging, in borders, in row gardens
Cultivars 'Blanche,' 'Doris,' 'Helen'
Hardiness Zone 3
Partners Geranium, gypsophila, veronica

Dianthus barbatus

FAMILY–CARYOPHYLLACEAE
COMMON NAME–SWEET WILLIAM

Origin Europe
Leaves Flat, broad, generally dense
Flowers Red, rose, and white in dense clusters to 3 in (7.5cm) across
Habit Mass of flowers to 18 in (45cm)
Season of Bloom Summer, spring
Culture Partial sun; moist soil
Propagation Self-seeding; plant up to 16 in (40cm) apart
Utilization A good border and edging plant
Hardiness Zone 6
Partners Geranium, thalictrum, veronica

Dianthus plumarius

FAMILY–CARYOPHYLLACEAE
COMMON NAME–PINKS

Origin Europe
Leaves Grassy, short, dark green, narrow, opposite
Flowers Pink, 1 in (2.5cm) across, usually fringed
Habit Forms mounds
Season of Bloom Summer
Culture Sun or partial shade; avoid soggy soil

Propagation Tip cuttings; plant up to 14 in (35cm) apart
Utilization Attractive in almost any area of the garden; as edging, in borders
Cultivars 'Evangeline,' 'Her Majesty'
Hardiness Zone 3
Partners Geranium, gypsophila, veronica

Dicentra spectabilis

FAMILY–PAPAVERACEAE
COMMON NAME–BLEEDING
HEART

Origin Japan
Leaves Feathery, divided
Flowers Pinkish-red, 1 in (2.5cm) long on a one-sided, arched stem
Habit Arching plant to 2 ft (60cm)
Season of Bloom Spring
Culture Sun or partial shade; well-drained soil

Propagation Most cuttings, division; plant up to 14 in (35cm) apart
Utilization Effective accent plant; good in woodland gardens
Hardiness Zone 2
Partners Myosotis, tulip

The natural, woodland garden (below) *is
enhanced in spring by the rich rose flowers of bleeding heart.*

Dictamnus fraxinella
rubra (purpureus)

FAMILY–RUTACEAE
COMMON NAME–GAS PLANT

Origin Europe, Asia
Leaves Glossy, pinnate, woody
Flowers Mauve-purple, 1 in (2.5cm) long
Habit Semierect to 3 ft (1m)
Season of Bloom Late spring
Culture Partial shade; well-drained soil
Propagation Seed; plant up to 20 in

(50cm) apart
Utilization Elegant in borders or drifts
Hardiness Zone 2
Partners Anemone, monarda, trollius
NOTE: Leaves can cause minor rash;
   handle with care

Dierama pulcherrimum

FAMILY–IRIDACEAE
COMMON NAME–WANDFLOWER

Origin South Africa
Leaves Grassy, evergreen
Flowers Lilac, pink
Habit Semierect
Season of Bloom Summer
Culture Full sun; well-drained soil

Propagation Seed; plant up to 12 in (30cm) apart
Utilization Graceful accent in any garden area
Hardiness Zone 5
Partners Rose, thalictrum

Digitalis grandiflorum (ambigua)

FAMILY–SCROPHULARIACEAE
COMMON NAME–FOXGLOVE

Origin Greece
Leaves Smooth, green, alternate, crowded
Flowers Yellow, 2 in (5cm) long
Habit Clump growth to 1 ft (30cm)
Season of Bloom Summer
Culture Partial sun; easily grown in almost any soil
Propagation Division, seed; plant up to 12 in (30cm) apart
Utilization Woodland garden area, fern garden
Cultivars 'Alba,' 'Foxy Miss'
Hardiness Zone 3
Partners Achillea, gypsophila, violet
NOTE: Parts of plant are poisonous if ingested

Doronicum caucasium (orientale)

FAMILY–COMPOSITAE
COMMON NAME–LEOPARD'S BANE

Origin Europe
Leaves Heart-shaped, toothed, basal
Flowers Yellow, daisylike
Habit Semierect to 2 ft (60cm)
Season of Bloom Early spring, summer
Culture Light shade; rich soil that drains readily

Propagation Division; plant up to 16 in (45cm) apart
Utilization Attractive cut flowers; good perennial border plant
Cultivars 'Miss Mason, 'Spring Beauty'
Hardiness Zone 3
Partners Bulbs, dicentra

Echinacea purpurea

FAMILY–COMPOSITAE
COMMON NAME–CONEFLOWER

Origin United States
Leaves Toothed, leafy, dark green, alternate
Flowers Purple shades, 3 in (7.5cm) across on tall stems
Habit Branching stems to 3 ft (1m)
Season of Bloom Summer
Culture Sun; rich, well-drained soil

Propagation Division; plant up to 18 in (45cm) apart
Utilization Good in garden beds and drifts; attractive cut flowers
Cultivars 'Shooting Star,' 'White Luster'
Hardiness Zone 3
Partners Helenium, hemerocalis, sidalcea

The gracefully drooping petals of coneflowers were as popular in grandmother's garden as they are today (below).

Epimedium niveum

FAMILY–BERBERIDACEAE
COMMON NAME–BISHOP'S HAT

Origin Hybrid
Leaves Cordate, scalloped edges, toothed in leaflets
Flowers White, .5 in (1.2cm) across
Habit Small, compact clumps
Season of Bloom Early spring
Culture Sun or shade in any reasonable soil

Propagation Division; plant up to 12 in (30cm) apart
Utilization Ground cover, good for edging
Hardiness Zone 5
Partners Delphinium, geranium, lobelia

Epimedium X versicolor

FAMILY–BERBERIDACEAE
COMMON NAME–BISHOP'S HAT

Origin Hybrid
Leaves Ovate, scalloped, toothed
Flowers Yellow, 1 in (2.5cm) across
Habit Sprawling, ground cover
Season of Bloom Early spring
Culture Partial sun; well-drained soil
Propagation Division; plant up to 12 in (30cm) apart
Utilization Good as edging and in borders, or as ground cover
Cultivars 'Sulphureum'
Hardiness Zone 5
Partners Delphinium, geranium, lobelia

Eremurus elwesii 'Albus'

FAMILY–LILIACAEA
COMMON NAME–DESERT CANDLE

Origin Persia
Leaves Fleshy, sword-shaped, dying down after flowering
Flowers Tall, towering, white flower spikes up to 6 ft (2m) tall
Habit Clump-forming, erect; plants die down and go dormant during most of summer and winter
Season of Bloom Spring, early summer
Culture Plant bulbs 8 in (20cm) deep, three feet apart, in fertile, well-drained loam soil in sun or partial shade
Propagation By division of bulblets
Utilization Good towering accent for the back of mixed perennial borders; best planted in a sheltered location against an evergreen hedge
Hardiness Zone 7, further north with protection
Partners Columbine, doronicum, gas plant, heuchera

Erigeron glaucus

FAMILY–COMPOSITAE
COMMON NAME–FLEABANE

Origin North America
Leaves Grayish green, basal
Flowers Mauve, daisylike, 2 in (5cm) across
Habit Forms dense clumps to 2 ft (60cm)
Season of Bloom Summer
Culture Sun; well-drained soil
Propagation Seed; plant up to 18 in (45cm) apart
Utilization Edging, borders
Hardiness Zone 6
Partners Campanula, chrysanthemum, veronica

Erigeron karvinskianus

FAMILY–COMPOSITAE
COMMON NAME–FLEABANE

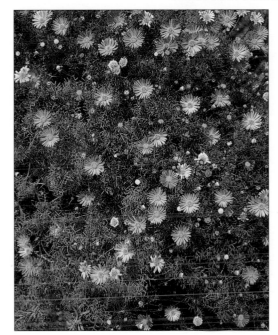

Origin Mexico
Leaves Grassy, basal, toothed
Flowers Pink-and-white
Habit Clump growth, forms masses of color to 1 ft (30cm)
Season of Bloom Summer
Culture Sun; well-drained soil
Propagation Division, seed; plant up to 18 in (45cm) apart
Utilization Use as border plant or in edging
Hardiness Zone 5
Partners Campanula, chrysanthemum, veronica

Eryngium X oliverianum

FAMILY–UMBELLIFERAE
COMMON NAME–SEA HOLLY

Origin Hybrid
Leaves Evergreen, long, narrow, cut or lobed, usually spiny
Flowers Prickly, blue flower heads with showy bracts
Habit Thistle-type, deeply lobed leaves
Season of Bloom Summer
Culture Sun; well-drained soil
Propagation Division, seed; plant up to 24 in (60cm) apart
Utilization Good for drying, can be used as an everlasting
Cultivars 'Peace'
Hardiness Zone 6
Partners Best by itself

Eucomis autumnalis

FAMILY–LILIACEAE
COMMON NAME–PINEAPPLE LILY

Origin South Africa
Leaves Limp, large, broad
Flowers Tiny greenish flowers on tall plumes
Habit Erect to 2 ft (60cm)
Season of Bloom Summer
Culture Shade; easily grown in moist soils
Propagation Division; plant up to 20 in (50cm) apart
Utilization Good potted plant; attractive vertical accent in perennial border
Hardiness Zone 10
Partners By itself as accent

Euphorbia epithymoides (polychroma)

FAMILY–EUPHORBIACEAE
COMMON NAME–CUSHION SPURGE

Origin Europe
Leaves Small, lanceolate
Flowers Dense masses of yellow clusters
Habit Forms clumps to 18 in (45cm)
Season of Bloom Spring
Culture Sun; well-drained soil
Propagation Division; plant up to 18 in (45cm) apart
Utilization Good in rock garden areas; effective background plant
Hardiness Zone 4
Partners Monarda, phlox, primula

Euphorbia lophogora

FAMILY–EUPHORBIACEAE
COMMON NAME–MILKWEED;
SPURGE

Origin Madagascar
Leaves Ovate, in tufts at edge of
branches
Flowers White or pink, dense
Habit Erect shrub to 2 ft (60cm)
Season of Bloom Summer
Culture Partial sun; well-drained soil
Propagation Seed; plant up to 18 in
(45cm) apart
Utilization Good background plant; fine
specimen by itself
Hardiness Zone 5
Partners Monarda, phlox

Euryops mauritanus

FAMILY–COMPOSITAE
COMMON NAME–FALSE DAISY

Origin South Africa
Leaves Alternate, crowned, lobed
Flowers Yellow, 3 in (7.5cm) across on
tall stems
Habit Grows in clumps to 18 in (45cm)
Season of Bloom Summer, fall
Culture Sun; moist well-drained soil
Propagation Division; plant up to 16 in
(40cm) apart
Utilization A good background plant;
attractive cut flowers
Hardiness Zone 9
Partners Gazania, gypsophila,
helianthus

Filipendula rubra

FAMILY–ROSACEAE
COMMON NAME–QUEEN OF THE
PRAIRIE

Origin North America
Leaves Featherlike, alternate, compound
Flowers Pink spires on tall stems
Habit Graceful, erect to 4 ft (1.2m)
Season of Bloom Summer
Culture Partial shade; well-drained soil
Propagation Division; plant up to 36 in (1m) apart
Utilization Excellent background plant
Cultivars 'Venusta'
Hardiness Zone 3
Partners Ajuga, arctotis, gaillardia

Filipendula vulgaris

FAMILY–ROSACEAE
COMMON NAME–DROPWORT,
MEADOWSWEET

Origin Native to Europe
Leaves Most are basal with a few on flower stems; pinnately compound, 6 to 12 in (15-30cm) long and 1 to 2 in (2.5-5cm) wide
Flowers White tinged with red on the outside, ¾ in (2cm) across, numerous 5 to 6 petalled small flowers arranged in a terminal panicle
Habit Mounded foliage above which rise 2 ft (60cm) tall flower stalks
Season of Bloom Late spring to early summer
Culture Sun or partial shade; fertile loam soil; will tolerate dry and infertile sites
Propagation Self seeds in abundance; also, by division.
Utilization Excellent in borders
Hardiness Zone 4
Partners Bearded iris, lily, ox-eye daisy; peony

Gaillardia X grandiflora

FAMILY–COMPOSITAE
COMMON NAME–
BLANKETFLOWER

Origin Hybrid
Leaves Small rosettes, soft in texture
Flowers Red to orange, 4 in (10cm)
  across on wiry stems
Habit Arching, graceful to 2 ft (60cm)
Season of Bloom Summer
Culture Sun; easily grown in most soils
Propagation Division; plant up to 18 in
  (45cm) apart
Utilization Good cut flower; effective
  mass of color in beds
Cultivars 'Burgundy,' 'Goblin'
Hardiness Zone 3
Partners Gypsophila, larkspur, salvia

Geranium dalmaticum

FAMILY–GERANIACEAE
COMMON NAME–GERANIUM

Origin Europe
Leaves Lobed, ferny, dissected
Flowers Small pinkish flowers in
  clusters
Habit Low growing, spreading
Season of Bloom Summer, fall
Culture Partial shade; moist soil
Propagation Division; plant up to 20 in
  (50cm) apart
Utilization Good in woodland or wild
  gardens
Hardiness Zone 5
Partners Fern, heuchera, hosta

Geranium endressii

FAMILY–GERANIACEAE
COMMON NAME–BLUE
CRANESBILL

Origin Hybrid
Leaves Alternate, stalked, round or lobed, sometimes fernlike
Flowers Blue-violet, 2 in (5cm) across, profuse
Habit To 12 in (30cm)
Season of Bloom Summer, fall
Culture Shade; moist soil

Propagation Division; plant up to 24 in (60cm) apart
Utilization Woodland garden, wild garden
Cultivars 'Johnson's Blue,' 'Wargrave Pink'
Hardiness Zone 4
Partners Fern, heuchera, hosta

Geranium psilostemon

FAMILY–GERANIACEAE
COMMON NAME–CRANESBILL

Origin Armenia
Leaves Dark green, deeply lobed
Flowers Rosy-red spotted black at the center, cup-shaped, 1½ in (3cm) across
Habit Bushy, spreading, up to 2 ft (60cm) high
Season of Bloom Summer
Culture Full sun; prefers well-drained, fertile loam soil
Propagation By division and by seed
Utilization Excellent highlights in mixed borders and massed for a groundcover effect
Hardiness Zone 5
Partners Daylilies, garden lilies, phlox, yellow loosestrife

Geranium sanguineum

FAMILY–GERANIACEAE
COMMON NAME–BLOOD
CRANESBILL

Origin Europe
Leaves Lobed, in mounds
Flowers Dense, reddish pink, 1 in
  (2.5cm) across
Habit Low growing to 12 in (30cm)
Season of Bloom Summer
Culture Partial sun; almost any soil
Propagation Division; plant up to 18 in
  (45cm) apart
Utilization Good for borders and wild
  gardens
Cultivars 'Album,' 'Lancastriense'
Hardiness Zone 4
Partners Aquilegia, cosmos

Geum quellyon

FAMILY–ROSACEAE
COMMON NAME–AVENS

Origin Chile
Leaves Small frills, lobed, basal leaves
  scattered along leaf blades
Flowers Yellow or orange on wiry stems
Habit Sprawling to 2 ft (60cm)
Season of Bloom Spring, summer
Culture Sun; well-drained soil
Propagation Division, seed; plant up to
  16 in (40cm) apart
Utilization Good in drifts and borders;
  showy in any area
Cultivars 'Borisii,' 'Fire Opal,'
  'Georgenberg'
Hardiness Zone 5
Partners Ageratum, campanula, phlox

Goniolimon tataricum
(Statice tatarica,
Limonium tatarica)

FAMILY–PLUMBAGINACEAE
COMMON NAME–GERMAN
STATICE

Origin Russia
Leaves Broadly lanceolate, 6 in (15cm) long or more
Flowers White or pale pink, small, massed in a dense, cloud-like mounded mass, the flowers have a papery texture valued for dried flower arrangements
Habit 18 in (45cm) tall
Season of Bloom Summer
Culture Full sun; fertile, loam soil
Propagation Mostly grown from seed, but also from division
Utilization Use in cutting gardens, mixed beds, and borders
Hardiness Zone 3
Partners Chinese lantern, money plant, sea lavender

Gypsophila paniculata

FAMILY–CAROPHYLLACEAE
COMMON NAME–BABY'S BREATH

Origin Europe
Leaves Small and inconspicuous, opposite
Flowers Tiny white or pink flowers in profusion
Habit Mounds of color, 1 to 2 ft (30 to 60cm) high
Season of Bloom Summer
Culture Partial sun; grows well in lime soil
Propagation Division; plant up to 16 in (40cm) apart
Utilization With spring bulbs, to fill empty space
Cultivars 'Early Snowball,' 'Snowflake'
Hardiness Zone 3
Partners Geranium, papaver, phlox

Hedychium gardneranum

FAMILY–ZINGIBERACEAE
COMMON NAME–KAHILI GINGER,
GINGER LILY

Origin Northern India
Leaves Sessile and lanceolate, up to 18 in (45cm) long and 6 in (15cm) wide
Flowers Light yellow flowers with red filaments, spikes to 18 in (45cm) long
Habit Erect with large stiff stems
Season of Bloom Summer
Culture Grown in greenhouses or outdoors in frostless areas, require rich soil and plenty of water
Propagation Division of rhizomes in mid-spring
Utilization Use in permanent beds or pools in tropics
Hardiness Zone 9
Partners Bird of paradise, canna, datura

Helenium autumnale

FAMILY–COMPOSITAE
COMMON NAME–SNEEZEWEED

Origin North America
Leaves Narrow, thin, alternate on stems
Flowers Yellow, daisylike
Habit Can get rangy and need staking, grows to 4 ft (1.2m)
Season of Bloom Summer, fall
Culture Sun; moist soil
Propagation Division; plant up to 14 in (35cm) apart
Utilization Backbone of a garden, use in borders, edging, for cutting
Cultivars 'Bruno,' 'Gypsy'
Hardiness Zone 3
Partners Ageratum, chrysanthemum, phlox

Hemerocallis Hybrid

FAMILY–LILIACEAE
COMMON NAME–DAYLILY

Origin Japan
Leaves Grassy, basal, narrow, bright green
Flowers Mainly soft shades of yellow and orange
Habit Medium to tall, to 3 ft (1m)
Season of Bloom Summer
Culture Sun or partial shade; almost any soil
Propagation Division; plant up to 28 in (70cm) apart
Utilization Exquisite as a border or background plant; good for bog gardens
Cultivars 'Johanna'
Hardiness Zones 3 to 9
Partners Delphinium, iris, platycodon

Heuchera sanguinea

FAMILY–SAXIFRAGACEAE
COMMON NAME–CORALBELLS

Origin United States
Leaves Maple-shaped, basal, lobed, hairy
Flowers Red, bell-shaped
Habit Rosettes, erect to 3 ft (1m)
Season of Bloom Summer
Culture Partial shade; even moist soil
Propagation Division; plant up to 12 in (30cm) apart
Utilization Makes a fine ground cover or garden filler; good in woodland gardens
Cultivars 'Chartreuse,' 'Chatterbox,' 'June Bride'
Hardiness Zone 3
Partners Campanula, veronica

Below: *While the annuals are still filling in during early summer, the hosta is making a magnificent statement.*

Hibiscus moscheutos

FAMILY–MALVACEAE
COMMON NAME–COMMON ROSE
MALLOW

Origin North America
Leaves Alternate, palmate, usually
  lobed
Flowers Large, bell-shaped, pink, to
  7 in (17cm) across
Habit Shrub growth to 7 ft (2.1m)
Season of Bloom Summer
Culture Sun; moist to wet soil
Propagation Division
Utilization Accent or background plant;
  good for hillsides
Cultivars 'Mallow Marvels'
Hardiness Zone 5
Partners Effective by itself

Hosta alba marginata
(sieboldii)

FAMILY–LILIACEAE
COMMON NAME–PLANTAIN LILY

Origin Japan
Leaves Spear-shaped with white edges;
  basal
Flowers White or violet
Habit Low-growing rosette
Season of Bloom Summer
Culture Partial shade; well-drained soil

Propagation Division; plant up to 16 in
  (40cm) apart
Utilization Good as border edging, or in
  woodland gardens
Hardiness Zone 3
Partners Effective by itself

Hosta seiboldiana

FAMILY–LILACEAE
COMMON NAME–PLANTAIN LILY

Origin Hybrid
Leaves Blue gray, basal
Flowers Pink, trumpet-shaped spires to 5 ft (1.6m)
Habit Vase-shaped, grows in clumps
Season of Bloom Summer
Culture Partial shade; well-drained soil

Propagation Division; plant up to 20 in (50cm) apart
Utilization Good border edging; also excellent as a singular accent, and in woodland gardens
Hardiness Zone 3
Partners Effective by itself

Hosta venusta

FAMILY–LILIACEAE
COMMON NAME–PLANTAIN LILY

Origin Japan
Leaves Lanceolate, green, basal
Flowers Mauve
Habit Dwarf, 6 in (15cm) high
Season of Bloom Summer
Culture Well-drained soil; partial shade

Propagation Division
Utilization Good for edging, as filler for perennial gardens; nice in woodsy settings
Hardiness Zone 3
Partners Effective by itself

Iberis sempervirens

FAMILY–CRUCIFERAE
COMMON NAME–CANDYTUFT

Origin Mediterranean region
Leaves Divided, alternate
Flowers White, in racemes
Habit Low growing, spreading to 12 in (30cm)
Season of Bloom Summer
Culture Partial sun; well-drained soil

Propagation Division
Utilization Good border and edging plant
Cultivars 'Autumn Snow,' 'Purity'
Hardiness Zone 4
Partners Dianthus, phlox

Incarvillea delavayi

FAMILY–BIGNONIACEAE
COMMON NAME–NONE

Origin China
Leaves Deeply divided foliage; pinnate, alternate
Flowers Red, trumpet-shaped flowers
Habit Clump growth
Season of Bloom Summer
Culture Sun; well-drained soil
Propagation Seed; plant up to 12 in (30cm) apart
Utilization Ideal for spot color in perennial gardens; good cut flowers
Hardiness Zone 5
Partners Epimedium, lobelia, primula

Inula ensifolia

FAMILY–COMPOSITAE
COMMON NAME–SUNRAY FLOWER

Origin Himalayas
Leaves Ferny, hairy, lanceolate
Flowers Yellow, daisylike to 2 in (5cm) across
Habit Scandent grower to 1 ft (30cm)
Season of Bloom Summer
Culture Sun; grows in any kind of soil
Propagation Division; plant up to 12 in (30cm) apart
Utilization Good in herb gardens or as background planting
Hardiness Zone 3
Partners Helianthus, rudbeckia, veronica

Iris germanica (bearded)

FAMILY–IRIDACEAE
COMMON NAME–BEARDED IRIS

Origin United States
Leaves Spatulate, gray-green, sword-shaped
Flowers Large, all colors
Habit Standard intermediate, tall from 2 to 6 ft (60cm to 2m)
Season of Bloom Summer
Culture Sun; well-drained soil
Propagation Division; plant up to 30 in (75cm) apart
Utilization Good in solitary beds or in drifts, attractive cut flowers
Hardiness Zone 3
Partners Effective by itself

Iris douglasiana

FAMILY–IRIDACEAE
COMMON NAME–PACIFIC COAST
IRIS

Origin Pacific Coast
Leaves Grassy, green, sword-shaped
Flowers Pastel colors
Habit Erect
Season of Bloom Summer, fall
Culture Full sun; sandy, acid soil
Propagation Division; plant up to 24 in (60cm) apart
Utilization Good in pond borders or as accent; attractive cut flowers
Hardiness Zone 5
Partners Effective by itself

Iris kaempferi (ensata)

FAMILY–IRIDACEAE
COMMON NAME–JAPANESE IRIS

Origin Japan, Asia
Leaves Ribbed, bright green, sword-shaped
Flowers Varied colors, mainly white and blue
Habit Erect to 3 ft (1m)
Season of Bloom Spring
Culture Sun; well-drained soil
Propagation Division; plant up to 18 in (45cm) apart
Utilization Good near water edges and in bog and woodland gardens
Cultivars 'Haku Bocan'
Hardiness Zone 5
Partners Effective by itself

Iris pallida

FAMILY–IRIDACEAE
COMMON NAME–SWEET IRIS,
ORRIS ROOT

Origin Native to Europe
Leaves Leaves up to 24 in (60cm) long, sword-blade shaped
Flowers Two to three flowers per spathe, fragrant bluish-purple, 3 in (7.5cm) long (with light beard). Three erect standards and three falls, similar to bearded iris.
Habit Rigid, erect, to 3 ft (1m) tall
Season of Bloom Late spring or early summer
Culture Full sun, average soil
Propagation Clump division in summer
Utilization Accent in border plantings
Hardiness Zone 6
Partners Astilbe, forget-me-not, marsh marigold, waterlily

*One of the most graceful perennials, Japanese iris (below)
resembles an orchid and grows best where water can reflect its beauty.*

Iris pseudacorus

FAMILY–IRIDACEAE
COMMON NAME–YELLOW FLAG

Origin Europe, Asia
Leaves Grassy, long, sword-shaped
Flowers Blue, purple or yellow
Habit Erect to 2 ft (60cm)
Season of Bloom Spring, summer
Culture Sun; moist soil
Propagation Division; plant up to 12 in (30cm) apart
Utilization Good for water gardens, pond borders, or soggy soil areas; attractive cut flowers
Hardiness Zone 5
Partners Effective by itself

Iris siberica

FAMILY–IRIDACEAE
COMMON NAME–SIBERIAN IRIS

Origin Europe, North Asia
Leaves Grassy, long, sword-shaped
Flowers Large, blue
Habit Clump growth to about 3 ft (1m)
Season of Bloom Late spring
Culture Sun; moist, rich, acid soil
Propagation Division; plant up to 18 in (45cm) apart
Utilization A good accent in woodsy areas and perennial gardens; attractive cut flowers
Hardiness Zone 3
Partners Peony, rose

Iris tectorum

FAMILY–IRIDACEAE
COMMON NAME–JAPANESE IRIS

Origin China
Leaves Narrow, long, ribbed, sword-shaped
Flowers Blue or white
Habit Erect to 1 ft (30cm)
Season of Bloom Late spring, summer
Culture Sun; sandy, dry, acid soil
Propagation Division; plant up to 12 in (30cm) apart
Utilization Good in woodsy gardens and perennial borders; attractive cut flowers
Hardiness Zone 5
Partners Effective by itself

Kniphofia (Tritoma) uvaria

FAMILY–LILIACEAE
COMMON NAME–RED-HOT POKER

Origin Cape Peninsula
Leaves Long, grassy, basal
Flowers Small orange flowers on tall spires
Habit Erect to 3 ft (1m)
Season of Bloom Summer, fall
Culture Sun; well-drained soil
Propagation Division; plant up to 24 in (60cm) apart
Utilization Good spashy color for background in gardens or as specimen planting
Cultivars 'Border Ballet,' 'Vanilla'
Hardiness Zone 6
Partners Chrysanthemum, gomphrena

Lamium maculatum

FAMILY–LABIATAE
COMMON NAME–DEAD NETTLE

Origin Europe
Leaves Opposite, stalked
Flowers White clusters, 1 in (2.5cm) long
Habit Low growing, in masses to 12 in (30cm)
Season of Bloom Spring, summer
Culture Partial sun; well-drained soil
Propagation Division; plant up to 12 in (30cm) apart
Utilization Good as ground cover or edging; effective foliage
Cultivars 'Alba,' 'White Nancy'
Hardiness Zone 4
Partners Delphinium, hemerocallis

Lavandula angustifolia

FAMILY–LABIATAE
COMMON NAME–LAVENDER

Origin Europe
Leaves Opposite with marginal teeth
Flowers Lavender, in clusters, .5 in (1.2cm) long
Habit Rosette growth, erect to 2 ft (60cm)
Season of Bloom Summer
Culture Partial sun; well-drained soil
Propagation Division; plant up to 20 in (50cm) apart
Utilization Makes fine hedges; good background planting
Cultivars 'Jean Davis,' 'Munstead Dwarf,' 'Twicket Purple'
Hardiness Zone 6
Partners Cerastium, lobelia, myosotis

Leonotis leonurus

FAMILY–LABIATAE
COMMON NAME–LION'S EAR

Origin South Africa
Leaves Serrate, oblong to 4 in (10cm)
Flowers Orange, tufted on tall stems
Habit Shrublike, erect to 6 ft (2m)
Season of Bloom Summer
Culture Sun; somewhat dry soil
Propagation Division; plant up to 24 in (60cm) apart
Utilization Good as a background or accent plant
Hardiness Zone 9
Partners Effective by itself

Leontopodium alpinum

FAMILY–COMPOSITAE
COMMON NAME–EDELWEISS

Origin Europe, Asia
Leaves Basal, alternate, gray, woolly on both sides
Flowers Yellow, 1 in (2.5cm) across, terminal borne
Habit Stems erect to 16 in (40cm)
Season of Bloom Summer
Culture Sun; needs sandy soil
Propagation Division; plant up to 12 in (30cm) apart
Utilization Good bedding or background plant
Hardiness Zone 4
Partners Hemerocallis, lobelia, phlox

Liatris pycnostachya

FAMILY–COMPOSITAE
COMMON NAME–KANSAS
GAYFEATHER

Origin Native to North America
Leaves Many (borne on stem), alternate lower leaves to 16 in (40cm) long, progressively reduced upward
Flowers Purple or pinkish
Habit Tall, to 5 ft (1.5m)
Season of Bloom Midsummer to late fall
Culture Sun or light shade in light soils
Propagation By seed, will flower from seed in two years
Utilization Attractive cut flower, good for drying, or in borders
Hardiness Zone 4 (tolerant of hot summers, suitable for southern areas)
Partners Daylily, coneflower, garden lily, rudbeckia

Liatris spicata 'Kobold'

FAMILY–COMPOSITAE
COMMON NAME–GAY FEATHER

Origin Hybrid
Leaves Ferny, alternate leaves on tall stems to 4 ft (1.2m)
Flowers Rosy purple or white frilly flowers
Habit Erect, mass grower
Season of Bloom Summer
Culture Full sun; rich, well-drained soil
Propagation Division; plant up to 12 in (30cm) apart
Utilization A good background plant; attractive cut flowers
Hardiness Zone 3
Partners Arabis, lampranthus, sedum

Ligularia przewalskii
(formerly Senecio)

FAMILY–COMPOSITAE
COMMON NAME–RAGWORT

Origin North China
Leaves Handsome, foliage wilts in hot sun even when sufficiently moist
Flowers Yellow, 4 to 6 ft (1.2-2m) tall
Habit Tall flower spikes over mounds of leaves
Season of Bloom Summer

Culture Full sun; humus-rich soil, abundant moisture
Propagation Division
Utilization Large accent in border or garden
Hardiness Zone 3
Partners Aruncus, hosta, forget-me-not, astilbe, rodgersia

Linum perenne

FAMILY–LINACEAE
COMMON NAME–BLUE FLAX,
PERENNIAL FLAX

Origin Native to Europe
Leaves Alternate, linear to lanceolate, 1 in (2.5cm) long
Flowers Blue, 1 in (2.5cm) across, individual flowers; short-lived, but profuse, blooms keep plant in flower
Habit Upright, 24 in (60cm) tall with arching stems
Season of Bloom Late spring and summer

Culture Not specialized—full sun or shade with a light, well-drained soil
Propagation Best by seed or cuttings (often self-sowing)
Utilization Good in rock gardens, perennial borders, or wild gardens
Hardiness Zone 5, excellent in Zone 8
Partners Geranium centranthus, poppy, Sweet William

Lirope muscari

FAMILY–LILIACEAE
COMMON NAME–MONDO GRASS;
LILYTURF

Origin East Asia
Leaves Dense tufts of dark, grasslike, shiny leaves
Flowers Bright violet
Habit Sprawling clumps with flowers raised above leaves
Season of Bloom Summer, fall
Culture Sun; well-drained soil
Propagation Division; plant up to 18 in (45cm) apart
Utilization Lawn plant, good ground cover
Cultivars 'Majestic'
Hardiness Zone 6
Partners Delphinium, helenium, rudbeckia

Perennials have a lot to offer. Some, like German statice, are pretty in the garden or in dried arrangements (below).

Lobelia cardinalis

FAMILY–CAMPANULACEAE
COMMON NAME–CARDINAL
FLOWER

Origin Eastern United States
Leaves Basal rosettes of green leaves
with toothed margins and leafy
stems; alternate
Flowers Red, 1 in (2.5cm) long on tall
spikes
Habit Erect to 3 to 4 ft (1 to 1.2m)
Season of Bloom Summer
Culture Partial shade; moist soil
Propagation Division; plant up to 12 in
(30cm) apart
Utilization Good border accent; excel-
lent for water gardens
Hardiness Zone 2
Partners Chrysanthemum, phlox

Lobelia siphilitica

FAMILY–CAMPANULACEAE
COMMON NAME–BLUE LOBELIA

Origin Eastern United States
Leaves Leafy rosettes, grassy foliage,
alternate
Flowers Blue, 1 in (2.5cm) long
Habit Erect to 3 ft (1m), forms drifts
Season of Bloom Summer
Culture Partial sun; will tolerate some-
what dry soil
Propagation Seed; plant up to 12 in
(30cm) apart
Utilization Good bog or background
plant
Hardiness Zone 4
Partners Delphinium, rose, rudbeckia

Lupinus polyphyllus

FAMILY–LEGUMINOSAE
COMMON NAME–WASHINGTON
LUPINE

Origin North America
Leaves Dense, 2 to 6 in (5 to 15cm),
  long, silky hairs underneath, gla-
  brous above
Flowers Blue, yellow, on tall spires
Habit Semierect to 3 ft (1m)
Season of Bloom Summer
Culture Full sun; well-drained soil
Propagation Seed; plant up to 24 in
  (60cm) apart
Utilization Good as background plants;
  effective color in gardens
Cultivars 'Russell Hybrids'
Hardiness Zone 3
Partners Artemesia, pyrethrum

Below: *Lupinus* x *hybrida*.

Lychnis chalcedonica

FAMILY–CARYOPHYLLACEAE
COMMON NAME–MALTESE CROSS,
JERUSALEM CROSS, SCARLET
LIGHTNING, LONDON PRIDE

Origin Native to Russia
Leaves Opposite, 2 to 4 in (5-10cm)
Flowers Vivid scarlet, dense terminal
head composed of 10 to 50 flowers,
flower heads 3 to 4 in (7.5-10cm) in
diameter
Habit Erect to 2 ft (60cm)
Season of Bloom Summer
Culture Sun or partial shade; moist,
well-drained soil with good fertility
Propagation Seed or division
Utilization Small massings in perennial
borders
Hardiness Zone 4
Partners Salvia 'East Friesland', Del-
phinium, yarrow

Lychnis coronaria

FAMILY–CAROPHYLLACEAE
COMMON NAME–ROSE CAMPION

Origin Southern Europe
Leaves Brilliantly colored or white
spear-shaped woolly leaves
Flowers Bright pink, rounded flowers
Habit Sprawling, basal clumps
Season of Bloom Summer
Culture Full sun; well-drained soil

Propagation Seed; plant up to 12 in
(30cm) apart
Utilization Good background color in
the perennial garden
Hardiness Zone 4
Partners Chrysanthemum, hemerocallis

*Where space allows, perennials such as
lupines can be grown in a wildflower meadow* (below).

Lysimachia clethroides

FAMILY–PRIMULACEAE
COMMON NAME–GOOSENECK
LOOSESTRIFE

Origin China, Japan
Leaves Smooth edged, spear-shaped, alternate
Flowers White flowers tightly packed on stems
Habit Grows in clumps to 3 ft (1m)
Season of Bloom Summer
Culture Partial sun; moist soil
Propagation Division; plant up to 24 in (60cm) apart
Utilization Handsome background plant; for mass display
Hardiness Zone 3
Partners Ajuga, gazania, hemerocallis, solidago

Lysimachia punctata

FAMILY–PRIMULACEAE
COMMON NAME–LOOSESTRIFE

Origin Asia Minor
Leaves Handsome, scalloped, spear-shaped
Flowers Whorls of yellow flowers
Habit Forms nice background foil, grows dense foliage to 3 ft (1m)
Season of Bloom Summer
Culture Partial sun; well-drained soil
Propagation Division; plant up to 24 in (60cm) apart
Utilization Good border plant; or use as accent
Hardiness Zone 5
Partners Gazania, hemerocallis

Macleaya cordata

FAMILY–PAPAVERACEAE
COMMON NAME–PLUME POPPY

Origin Asia
Leaves Alternate, gray-green with silver underneath, dense
Flowers Small pink or white flowers, in a terminal panicle
Habit Erect to 4 ft (1.2m)
Season of Bloom Summer
Culture Partial shade; well-drained soil
Propagation Division; plant up to 24 in (60cm) apart
Utilization Good background or bedding plant
Hardiness Zone 4
Partners Fern, hosta, phlox

Malva moschata

FAMILY–MALVACEAE
COMMON NAME–MALLOW

Origin Europe
Leaves Fernlike, dark green, alternate
Flowers Pink, 3 in (7.5cm) across on upper leaf axils
Habit Scandent grower to 3 ft (1m)
Season of Bloom Summer, fall
Culture Sun; moist well-drained soil
Propagation Cuttings, seed; plant up to 24 in (60cm) apart
Utilization Good edging plant; effective mass of color
Hardiness Zone 4
Partners Best by itself

Monarda didyma

FAMILY–LABIATAE
COMMON NAME–BEE BALM

Origin North America
Leaves Opposite, ovate leaves 3 to 6 in
   (7.5 to 15cm) long, downy underside
Flowers Terminal clusters of red flowers
Habit Dense clumps to 3 ft (1m)
Season of Bloom Summer
Culture Partial shade; moist soil
Propagation Division; plant up to 18 in
(45cm) apart
Utilization Great plant for perennial
   borders; super color
Cultivars 'Cambridge Scarlet,'
   'Croftway Pink'
Hardiness Zone 4
Partners Heuchera, phlox, trollius

Nepeta mussinii

FAMILY–LABIATAE
COMMON NAME–ORNAMENTAL
CATMINT

Origin Native to Europe
Leaves Blue-green, lanceolate, narrow,
   pointed
Flowers Blue, arranged in clusters
   along slender stems
Habit Bushy, erect; can create a uniform
   hedge effect
Season of Bloom Early summer
Culture Full sun; moist, loam soil
Propagation By seed and division
Utilization Massed in a border and as a
   highlight in mixed planting of peren-
   nials; popular in herb gardens
Hardiness Zone 4
Partners Daylily, lamb's ear, ox-eye
   daisy

Oenothera missouriensis

FAMILY–ONAGRACEAE
COMMON NAME–OZARK
SUNDROP

Origin Southern United States
Leaves Stems prostrate, dark green, narrow, with silver midribs
Flowers Lemon yellow, graceful flowers on leafy stems
Habit Low mounds that spread rapidly
Season of Bloom Summer, fall
Culture Sun; well-drained soil
Propagation Seed; plant up to 20 in (50cm) apart
Utilization Good for edging a path or walk
Hardiness Zone 4
Partners Chrysanthemum, delphinium, violet

Oenothera speciosa

FAMILY–ONAGRACEAE
COMMON NAME–EVENING
PRIMROSE

Origin North America
Leaves Small, ovoid, toothed, gray-green
Flowers Pink or white, 2 in (5cm) across
Habit Low growing to 8 in (20cm)
Season of Bloom Summer
Culture Sun; well-drained soil
Propagation Seed; plant up to 20 in (50cm) apart
Utilization Good edging plant for paths and walks
Cultivars 'Rosea'
Hardiness Zone 5
Partners Arabis, aster, gazania

Oenothera tetragona

FAMILY–ONAGRACEAE
COMMON NAME–SUNDROP

Origin North America
Leaves Flat, small, lanceolate
Flowers Yellow, saucer-shaped
Habit Dense, spreading mats of flat-
  leaved rosettes
Season of Bloom Summer
Culture Sun; well-drained soil
Propagation Division; plant up to 12 in
  (30cm) apart
Utilization Edging plant only, not for
  drifts or borders
Cultivars 'Fireworks,' 'Illumination'
Hardiness Zone 4
Partners Arabis, aster, gazania

Opuntia humifusa

FAMILY–CACTACAEA
COMMON NAME–HARDY PRICKLY PEAR

Origin Eastern USA
Leaves Thick, succulent, oval pads covered with sharp spines
Flowers Yellow with orange centers surrounding a yellow, powdery cluster of
  stamens, up to 3 in (7.5cm) across.
  Petals have a shimmering, satin-like
  sheen.
Habit Sprawling, ground-hugging
  plants, 8 in (20cm) high
Season of Bloom Late spring; fruits
  ripen in fall, persist through winter
Culture Full sun; well-drained, sandy
  soil; will tolerate high heat and
  drought
Propagation By division or leaf cuttings
Utilization Good as edging and ground
  cover, especially dry, sunny slopes,
  rock gardens, and dry walls
Hardiness Zone 5
Partners Echeveria, euphorbia, sedum,
  yucca

An informal early-summer perennial garden (below) can combine peonies with other perennials and bowers of roses.

Paeonia officinalis

FAMILY–PAEONIACEAE
COMMON NAME–PEONY

Origin Europe
Leaves Deeply cut into narrow elliptical segments, 3 to 4 in. (7.5 to 10cm) long, glabrous above, pubescent below
Flowers White, pink or red, 4 to 5 in (10 to 12cm) across
Habit Shrub
Season of Bloom Summer

Culture Sun; fertile, well-drained soil; needs feeding
Propagation Division; plant up to 24 in (60cm) apart
Utilization Flower beds, woodland gardens, cut flowers
Cultivars 'Rubra Plena'
Hardiness Zone 2
Partners Ajuga, iberis, myosotis

Paeonia suffruticosa

FAMILY–PAEONIACEAE
COMMON NAME–TREE PEONY

Origin China
Leaves Pinnate leaflets, divided, with hairs along midrib
Flowers Pink or white, 6 to 8 in (15 to 20cm) across
Habit Shrub to 4 ft (1.2m) (not a tree)
Season of Bloom Summer
Culture Partial sun; well-drained soil; needs feeding
Propagation Division; plant up to 24 in (60cm) apart
Utilization Beautiful in flower beds; attractive cut flowers
Hardiness Zone 2
Partners Ajuga, arabis, myosotis

Papaver orientale

FAMILY–PAPAVERACEAE
COMMON NAME–ORIENTAL POPPY

Origin Southwest Asia
Leaves Pinnately dissected, lanceolate or oblong
Flowers Red, open cups with black centers, ruffled edges
Habit Clump growth, erect to 3 ft (1m)
Season of Bloom Spring, summer
Culture Partial sun; well-drained soil

Propagation Root cuttings; plant up to 24 in (60cm) apart
Utilization In perennial beds or as accents near walls or fences; good as cut flowers
Cultivars 'Big Jim,' 'Harvest Moon'
Hardiness Zone 3
Partners Dianthus, phlox, rudbeckia

Penstemon gloxinioides

FAMILY–SCROPHULARIACEAE
COMMON NAME–PENSTEMON

Origin Mexico
Leaves Lanceolate to ovate, 4 in (10cm) long
Flowers Crimson, 2 in (5cm) long on tall stems
Habit Mass of color, erect to 3 ft (1m)
Season of Bloom Summer, fall
Culture Partial sun; well-drained soil
Propagation Division; plant up to 20 in (50cm) apart
Utilization Good bedding plant; effective vertical accent
Cultivars 'Firebird,' 'Huntington Pink,' 'Miss Leonard', 'Ruby King'
Hardiness Zone 9
Partners Phlox, platycodon, rudbekia

Phlox divaricata

FAMILY–POLEMONIACEAE
COMMON NAME–BLUE PHLOX

Origin North America
Leaves Elliptical leaves, 2 in (5cm) long
Flowers Blue, 1 in (2.5cm) across in loose clusters
Habit Mass growth to 6 in (15cm) high
Season of Bloom Spring
Culture Partial shade; moist soil

Propagation Rooted cuttings, seeds; plant up to 16 in (40cm) apart
Utilization Good in wildflower gardens or shaded areas; fragrant
Cultivars 'Fuller's White,' 'Laphamii'
Hardiness Zone 3
Partners Primula, pulmonaria

Phlox paniculata

FAMILY–POLEMONIACEAE
COMMON NAME–BORDER PHLOX

Origin North America
Leaves Papery, lanceolate or ovate, 4 in (10cm) long
Flowers Small, pink or purple, in spreading clusters
Habit Forms clumps to 4 ft (1.2m)
Season of Bloom Summer, fall
Culture Some sun; good, porous soil;

plenty of water
Propagation Rooted cuttings, seed; plant up to 20 in (50cm) apart
Utilization Used for borders, fragrance
Cultivars 'Amethyst,' 'Bright Eyes,' 'Thundercloud,' 'Pink Petticoat'
Hardiness Zone 4
Partners Aster, hemerocallis, phlox

Phlox subulata

FAMILY–POLEMONIACEAE
COMMON NAME–MOSS PINK

Origin North America
Leaves Long, dense, linear to 1 in (2.5cm)
Flowers Pink, blue or white, 1 in (2.5cm) across
Habit Mat-forming; prostrate to 5 in (12.5cm)
Season of Bloom Spring
Culture Partial sun; rich, well-drained soil
Propagation Rooted cuttings; plant up to 20 in (50cm) apart
Utilization Good ground cover or edging plant; fragrant
Cultivars 'Mountain Pink,' 'Twinkle Mix'
Hardiness Zone 3
Partners Aster, hemerocallis, phlox

Below: *A garden gazebo accents this midsummer garden where phlox thrives.*

Phormium tenax variegatum

FAMILY–LILIACEAE
COMMON NAME–NEW ZEALAND
FLAX

Origin New Zealand
Leaves Leathery, tough, outlined white, 9 ft (2.7m) long, 5 in (12.5cm) across
Flowers Pale red, 2 in (5cm) long on tall stems
Habit Large rosette
Season of Bloom Summer
Culture Sun; plenty of water
Propagation Division; plant up to 36 in (1m) apart
Utilization Accent plant where bold foliage is needed
Hardiness Zone 4
Partners Best as specimen plant

Platycodon grandiflorus

FAMILY–CAMPANULACEAE
COMMON NAME–
BALLOONFLOWER

Origin Far East
Leaves Blue-green, arranged up stem
Flowers Blue or white, wide, cup-shaped
Habit Compact clumps
Season of Bloom Summer
Culture Sun; thrives in fertile, acid soil
Propagation Seed; plant up to 18 in (45cm) apart
Utilization Good bedding plant; nice cut flower
Cultivars 'Albus,' 'Blue,' 'Shell Pink'
Hardiness Zone 3
Partners Chrysanthemum, coreopsis, lobelia

Potentilla verna 'Aurea'

FAMILY–ROSACEAE
COMMON NAME–CINQUEFOIL

Origin Europe
Leaves Digitate, toothed leaflets
Flowers Yellow
Habit Clump growth to 1 ft (30cm)
Season of Bloom Summer
Culture Sun; well-drained soil
Propagation Rooted cuttings; plant up to 20 in (50cm) apart
Utilization Good border plant; bright color
Cultivars 'Day Dawn'
Hardiness Zone 4
Partners Dianthus, rudbeckia, veronica

Primula X polyanthus

FAMILY–PRIMULACEAE
COMMON NAME–GERMAN
PRIMULA

Origin China
Leaves Ovate, elliptical foliage, scalloped
Flowers Lilac or pink in rounded heads
Habit Growing in dense clumps to 1 ft (30cm)
Season of Bloom Spring
Culture Partial shade; well-drained soil
Propagation Cool seeds and start indoors in fall; plant up to 18 in (45cm) apart
Utilization Useful in rock gardens and borders
Hardiness Zone 4
Partners Coreopsis, gerbera
NOTE: Leaves can produce rash on skin; handle with gloves.

Primula vulgaris

FAMILY–PRIMULACEAE
COMMON NAME–ENGLISH
PRIMROSE

Origin Europe
Leaves Long, wrinkled, toothed, paddle-shaped, obovate to 10 in (25cm)
Flowers Yellow, purple, or blue; many or few
Habit Rosette growth
Season of Bloom Spring
Culture Partial sun; well-drained soil
Propagation Seed; plant up to 18 in (45cm) apart
Utilization Good bedding or container plant
Hardiness Zone 3
Partners Lobelia, monarda, trollius

Pulmonaria angustifolia

FAMILY–BORAGINACEAE
COMMON NAME–BLUE
LUNGWORT

Origin Europe, Asia
Leaves Green or white spotted, ovate, pointed, 5 in (12.5cm) long
Flowers Blue, 1 in (2.5cm) long in clusters
Habit Mat, growing to 7 in (17.5cm)
Season of Bloom Spring
Culture Shade; rich soil
Propagation Division; plant up to 18 in (45cm) apart
Utilization In woodland gardens; good edging plant
Cultivars 'Aurea,' 'Lutea,' 'Salmon Glory'
Hardiness Zone 3
Partners Arabis, campanula, cerastium

Pyrethrum roseum (Chrysanthemum coccineum)

FAMILY–COMPOSITAE
COMMON NAME–PAINTED DAISY

Origin Europe
Leaves Usually divided, fern-like, alternate
Flowers Large pink flower heads
Habit Forms clumps, erect to 2 ft (60cm)
Season of Bloom Summer
Culture Sun; well-drained soil
Propagation Seed; plant up to 18 in (45cm) apart
Utilization Good background plant; fine bedding plant
Hardiness Zone 4
Partners Dianthus, gypsophila, veronica

Rehmannia angulata

FAMILY–GESNERICEAE
COMMON NAME–NONE

Origin China
Leaves Basal rosette, alternating on erect stems
Flowers Pink
Habit Upright clumps to 4 ft (1.2m)
Season of Bloom Summer
Culture Partial sun; well-drained soil
Propagation Division; plant up to 20 in (50cm) apart
Utilization Background planting
Hardiness Zone 4
Partners Arabis, campanula, phlox

Romneya coulteri

FAMILY–PAPAVERACEAE
COMMON NAME–TREE POPPY

Origin California
Leaves Pinnately divided, 4 in (10cm) long
Flowers White, large and floppy
Habit Shrublike to 6 ft (2m)
Season of Bloom Summer
Culture Sun; plenty of water; will tolerate poor soil
Propagation Seed, division; plant up to 20 in (50 cm) apart
Utilization Fine accent plant; good when massed for color
Hardiness Zone 5
Partners Effective by itself

Rosmarinus officinalis

FAMILY–LABIATAE
COMMON NAME–ROSEMARY

Origin Spain
Leaves Leathery, .5 in (1.2cm), obtuse
Flowers Pale blue, pink
Habit Shrub
Season of Bloom Spring
Culture Sun; somewhat dry soil
Propagation Division; plant up to 20 in (50cm) apart
Utilization Good for rock gardens and for trailing
Hardiness Zone 6
Partners Coreopsis, cosmos

Rodgersia aesculifolia

FAMILY–SAXIFRAGACEAE
COMMON NAME–
RODGERSFLOWER

Origin China
Leaves Dark green, heavily veined, re
sembling horse chestnut leaves
Flowers White, in clusters forming
handsome plumes similar in appear-
ance to astilbe
Habit Bushy, spreading to 6 ft (2m) high
Season of Bloom Early summer

Culture Partial shade; moist, fertile
loam soil
Propagation By division
Utilization Mostly used along pond
margins and stream banks
Hardiness Zone 5
Partners Astilbe, Siberian iris, yellow
flag iris

Below: *Rodgersia aesculifolia.*

Rudbeckia fulgida

FAMILY–COMPOSITAE
COMMON NAME–BLACK-EYED
SUSAN

Origin North America
Leaves Lanceolate to ovate, serrated
Flowers Yellow, daisylike, 2 in (5cm)
  across
Habit Clump growth
Season of Bloom Summer, fall
Culture Sun; rich, moist soil
Propagation Division; plant up to 12 in
  (30cm) apart
Utilization Effective bedding plant;
  good in woodland gardens
Cultivars 'Goldsturm'
Hardiness Zone 3
Partners Chrysanthemum, phlox,
  veronica

*Once a roadside plant, black-eyed Susan has, like
other perennials, been improved as a garden variety* (below).

Satureja montana

FAMILY–LABIATAE
COMMON NAME–WINTER SAVORY

Origin Mediterranean area
Leaves Linear to 1 in (2.5cm) long, .5 in (1.2cm) wide
Flowers White or pink
Habit Shrublike growth to 6 to 12 in (15 to 30cm)
Season of Bloom Summer
Culture Sun; moist soil
Propagation Division; plant up to 16 in (40cm) apart
Utilization In herb gardens; good border and edging plant
Hardiness Zone 3
Partners Aster, coreopsis, cosmos

Below: *Winter savory is one of several perennials, like rosemary and thyme, that can be planted in a kitchen garden.*

Scabiosa caucasica

FAMILY–DIPSACACEAE
COMMON NAME–PINCUSHION
FLOWER

Origin Africa, Asia, Europe
Leaves Opposite, dissected
Flowers Blue or white, 2 in (5cm) across
Habit Clump growth to 2 ft (60cm)
Season of Bloom Summer
Culture Sun; rich, well-drained soil
Propagation Division; plant up to 16 in (40cm) apart
Utilization Good garden plants in almost any situation; attractive cut flower
Cultivars 'Blue Perfection'
Hardiness Zone 3
Partners Aster, lobelia, phlox

Sedum spectabile

FAMILY–CRASSULACEAE
COMMON NAME–STONECROP

Origin S.W. Asia
Leaves Fleshy, gray-green clumps of somewhat toothed leaves, 3 in (7.5cm) long, 2 in (5cm) wide
Flowers Clusters of pink flowers
Habit Shrub
Season of Bloom Summer
Culture Sun; well-drained soil
Propagation Division, cuttings; plant up to 18 in (45cm) apart
Utilization Handsome edging plant; good in rock gardens
Cultivars 'Brilliant'
Hardiness Zone 3
Partners Ajuga, iberis

Sidalcea malvaeflora

FAMILY–MALVACEAE
COMMON
NAME–CHECKERBLOOM

Origin North America
Leaves Rounded, alternate, palmately lobed
Flowers Pink, 1 in (2.5cm) across on spires
Habit Stems erect to 3 ft (1m)
Season of Bloom Summer
Culture Sun; well-drained soil
Propagation Division; plant up to 24 in (60cm) apart
Utilization Good border plant; effective in drifts; mass for color accent
Hardiness Zone 4
Partners Chrysanthemum, phlox

Sisyrinchium bellum

FAMILY–IRIDACEAE
COMMON NAME–BLUE-EYED
GRASS

Origin North America
Leaves Grasslike, narrow, basal
Flowers Violet flowers, .75 in (1.9cm)
Habit Clump forming
Season of Bloom Summer
Culture Sun; will grow in most soils

Propagation Seeds; plant up to 8 in (20cm) apart
Utilization Good accent or background plant; spot color
Hardiness Zone 7
Partners Anemone, coreopsis, primula

Solidago hybrida
'Peter Pan'

FAMILY–COMPOSITAE
COMMON NAME–GOLDENROD

Origin Cross between species native to North America

Leaves Bright green, pointed, spear-shaped

Flowers Bright golden-yellow, arranged in clusters to form a plume

Habit Clump-forming, erect; 'Peter Pan', a dwarf, grows 2 ft (60cm) high

Season of Bloom Late summer

Culture Partial shade; moist, fertile soil

Propagation By division

Utilization Highlights in mixed borders

Hardiness Zone 4

Partners Aster, cardinalflower, lythrum, monarda

Stachys byzantina

FAMILY–LABIATAE
COMMON NAME–BETONY; LAMB'S
EARS

Origin Asia, Turkey

Leaves Silvery mats of leaves

Flowers Woolly spires of small purple flowers

Habit Mounds of foliage to 12 in (30cm)

Season of Bloom Summer

Culture Sun; will tolerate poor soil

Propagation Division; plant up to 16 in (40cm) apart

Utilization Good accent plant; effective foliage

Cultivars 'Silver Carpet'

Hardiness Zone 4

Partners Cosmos, lobelia, phlox

Stachys grandiflora
(Stachys macrantha)

FAMILY–LABIATAE (MINT)
COMMON NAME–BIG BETONY

Origin Native to the Caucasus Mountains

Leaves Stems are "square" (four-angled) and leaves are opposite. Two types of foliage: basal leaves are long-petioled, stem leaves are smaller and sessile; leaves and stems are hairy, leaves are wrinkled in appearance

Flowers Violet-purple and arranged in whorls, equally spaced on stiff stems

Habit 18 in (45cm) tall rosette-forming perennial

Season of Bloom Late spring to early summer

Culture Full sun; average, well-drained soil

Propagation Clump division or seed

Utilization Excellent in borders

Hardiness Zone 4

Partners Bearded iris, gas plant, ox-eye daisy, poppy

Stokesia laevis (cyanea)

FAMILY–COMPOSITAE
COMMON NAME–STOKE'S ASTER

Origin North America

Leaves Spiny, toothed at base; oblong to 8 in (20cm)

Flowers Blue flowers in tight heads

Habit Forms clumps, grows to 2 ft (60cm)

Season of Bloom Summer, fall

Culture Sun; light, well-drained soil

Propagation Seed, division; plant up to 18 in (45cm) apart

Utilization Something different for front of border; good for edging; attractive cut flowers

Cultivars 'Blue Moon'

Hardiness Zone 5

Partners Antirrhinum, chrysanthemum, phlox

Symphytum officinale

FAMILY–BORAGINACEAE
COMMON NAME–NONE

Origin Caucasus
Leaves Oblong, covered with hairs
Flowers Purple or rose
Habit Low growing, forms mats
Season of Bloom Summer
Culture Shade; wet soil

Propagation Division; plant up to 24 in (60cm) apart
Utilization Ground cover for cool places
Hardiness Zone 4
Partners Arabis, cerastium, solidago

Teucrium chamaedrys

FAMILY–LABIATAE
COMMON NAME–GERMANDER

Origin Europe, southwest Asia
Leaves Oblong, dense, deeply serrated
Flowers Pale blue, usually spotted, loose spikes
Habit Dwarf shrub to 2 ft (60cm)
Season of Bloom Summer
Culture Sun; well-drained soil

Propagation Division; plant up to 30 in (75cm) apart
Utilization Effective background plant; good foliage effect
Hardiness Zone 4
Partners Lobelia, phlox, solidago

Thermopsis caroliniana

FAMILY–LEGUMINOSAE
COMMON NAME–PERENNIAL
LUPINE, CAROLINA LUPINE

Origin Eastern seaboard of North America, particularly the Carolinas

Leaves Lupinelike, multiple clover-type leaflets

Flowers Yellow, pealike, arranged in an erect spire

Habit Clump-forming, bushy, erect to 3 to 4 ft (1-1.2m) high

Season of Bloom Early summer

Culture Full sun; deep, well-drained soil

Propagation From seeds, which need soaking overnight to hasten germination

Utilization Massed on slopes for erosion control; also singly as background highlights in mixed borders

Hardiness Zone 4

Partners Butterfly weed, globe bell flowers, iris

Tigrida pavonia

FAMILY–IRIDACEAE
COMMON NAME–PEACOCK
FLOWER

Origin Mexico

Leaves Ribbed, green, fan-shaped

Flowers Orange or red with markings

Habit Erect to 3 ft (1m)

Season of Bloom Summer

Culture Sun; well-drained soil

Propagation Division; plant up to 10 in (25cm) apart

Utilization Good in rock gardens; effective background plants

Hardiness Zone 5

Partners Coreopsis, delphinium, phlox

Tradescantia virginiana

FAMILY–COMMELINACEAE
COMMON NAME–SPIDERWORT,
WIDOW'S TEARS

Origin Eastern North America
Leaves Narrow, strap-like, 6 to 14 in (15-35cm) long, dull green
Flowers Usually blue, 1 to 2 in (2.5-5cm) across, three-petalled
Habit Erect, branching, to 3 ft (1m) tall
Season of Bloom Late spring to mid-autumn
Culture Shade, partial shade, shade or sun; good garden soil or compost
Propagation By division in spring
Utilization Good in borders, occasionally used in containers
Hardiness Zone 5
Partners Daylily, rudbeckia

Tricyrtis hirta

FAMILY–LILIACEAE
COMMON NAME–TOAD LILY

Origin Japan
Leaves Fuzzy, alternate, along hairy, un-branched, upright stems
Flowers Mauve or spotted purple in clusters in leaf axils
Habit Clump growth to 2 ft (60cm)
Season of Bloom Fall
Culture Sun; well-drained soil
Propagation Division, seed; plant up to 20 in (50cm) apart
Utilization Use for late-season color
Hardiness Zone 5
Partners Cerastium, lobelia, trollius

Trollius europaeus

FAMILY–RANUNCULACEAE
COMMON NAME–GLOBEFLOWER

Origin Europe
Leaves Dark green, toothed, lobed
Flowers Daisylike, yellow, 2 in (5cm) across, globe-shaped
Habit Somewhat erect to 2 ft (60cm)
Season of Bloom Summer
Culture Partial shade; moist boggy soil

Propagation Division; plant up to 18 in (45cm) apart
Utilization Good in water and woodland gardens
Cultivars 'Superbus'
Hardiness Zone 6
Partners Ferns, hostas

Vallota purpurea

FAMILY–AMARYLLIDACEAE
COMMON NAME–SCARBOROUGH
LILY

Origin S. Africa
Leaves Strap-shaped dark green leaves
Flowers Vivid orange-red, lilylike flowers
Habit Erect to 16 in (40cm), straight stems
Season of Bloom Summer

Culture Partial sun; well-drained soil
Propagation Division in fall; plant up to 10 in (25cm) apart
Utilization Use as accent plant or fill-in for borders
Hardiness Zone 9
Partners Cerastium, mirabilis, phlox

Verbena venosa (rigida)

FAMILY–VERBENACEAE
COMMON NAME–VERVAIN

Origin South America
Leaves Rough, dark green, oblong, toothed
Flowers Tiny lavender blue or red flowers
Habit Erect to 2 ft (60cm)
Season of Bloom Summer, fall
Culture Sun; well-drained soil

Propagation Division, seed; plant up to 12 in (30cm) apart
Utilization Good bedding plant; useful late flowering plant
Cultivars 'Glowing Violet,' 'Derby'
Hardiness Zone 7
Partners Asclepias, coreopsis, dianthus

*Rock gardens and sunny borders are good sites
for low-growing perennials such as verbena (below).*

Veronica latifolia

FAMILY–SCROPHULARIACEAE
COMMON NAME–SPEEDWELL

Origin New Zealand
Leaves Ovate, toothed
Flowers Small, blue-rose flowers from upper leaf axils
Habit Forms clumps erect to 2 ft (60cm)
Season of Bloom Summer
Culture Sun; well-drained soil
Propagation Division; plant up to 16 in (40cm) apart
Utilization Good in flower gardens and for borders
Cultivars 'Crater Lake,' 'Royal Blue'
Hardiness Zone 4
Partners Gypsophila, helianthus, yucca

Viola cornuta

FAMILY–VIOLACEAE
COMMON NAME–VIOLET

Origin Pyrenees
Leaves Small, bright green
Flowers Deep violet, yellow, or red in masses
Habit Low-growing rosettes
Season of Bloom Summer
Culture Shade; well-drained soil
Propagation Division, seed; plant up to 18 in (45cm) apart
Utilization Good in shady areas; effective ground cover
Cultivars Many
Hardiness Zone 5
Partners Effective by itself in mass

Appendix I

COMMON & BOTANICAL NAME CHARTS

Botanical–Common Name Chart

Botanical Name	Common Name
A	
Acanthus mollis	Bear's Breech
Acanthus spinosa	
Achillea filipendula	Fern-leaved Yarrow
Achillea f. 'Coronation Gold'	
Achillea millefolium 'Fire King'	Common Yarrrow
Achillea millefolium roseum	Pink-flowered Yarrow
Achillea ptarmica	Sneezeweed
Adenophora confusa	Bellflower
Ajuga reptans	Bugleweed
Allium schoenoprasum	Chives
Alstroemaria pulchella	Peruvian Lily
Anchusa myosotidiflora	Alkane
Aneomone x *hybrida*	Windflower
Aquilegia alpina	Columbine
Aquilegia a. 'Harebell'	Columbine
Aquilegia a. 'Crimson Star'	Columbine
Arabis albida (caucasica)	White Rockcress
Armeria maritima	Sea Pink; Thrift

*Plumed astilbe, pretty fresh or dried, is available
in shades of pink, red, white, and salmon* (below).

Artemesia schmidtiania	Mugwort; Silver Mound
Aster x *frikartii*	Aster
Aster x *novae-angliae*	Michaelmas Daisy; New England Aster
Astilbe x *arendsii*	Goat's Beard
Astilbe a. 'Fanal'	Goat's Beard
Astilbe a. 'Federsee'	Goat's Beard
Astilbe taquetti 'Superba'	Goat's Beard
Astrantia major	Masterwort
Aubretia deltoidea	Rockcress
Aurinia saxatilis	Basket-of-Gold

B

Baptisia australis	False Indigo
Bergenia cordifolia (white)	Heartleaf Bergenia
Bergenia cordifolia (pink)	Heartleaf Bergenia

C

Campanula glomerata	Bellflower
Campanula persicifolia 'White Star'	Peach-leaved Bellflower
Catananche caerulea	Cupid's Dart
Catharanthus roseus	Periwinkle
Centaurea cineraria	Dusty Miller
Centaurea macrocephala	Knapweed
Centaurea montana	Mountain Bluet
Centranthus (Valerian) ruber	Red Valerian
Cerastium tomentosum	Snow-in-summer
Chrysanthemum Coronarium	Crown Daisy
Chrysanthemum i. 'Star Gazer'	Cushion Mum
Chrysanthemum x *morifolium*	Chrysanthemum
Chrysanthemum nipponicum	Nippon Daisy
Chrysanthemum parthenium	Feverfew
Chrysogonum virginiana	Golden Star
Clematis recta	Ground Clematis
Coreopsis grandiflora 'Sunray'	Bigflower Coreopsis
Coreopsis verticillata	Threadleaf Coreopsis
Coreopsis v. 'Moonbeam'	Threadleaf Coreopsis
Crassula falcata	Scarlet Paintbrush

Crocosmia (montbretia) crocosmiflora	Montebretia
Crocosmia (montbretia) masonorum	Montebretia
Cyclamen coum	Shooting Star
Cyclamen repandum	Persian Violet

Below: *Some perennials, such as feverfew, easily self-sow and quickly fill in large areas.*

The flowers of bleeding heart (below) *gracefully droop from the undersides of arching branches.*

D

Delphinium elatum	Candle Larkspur
Delphinium x *belladonna*	Larkspur
Dianthus x *allwoodii*	Pink Carnation
Dianthus barbatus	Sweet William
Dianthus plumarius	Pinks
Dicentra spectabilis	Bleeding Heart
Dictamus fraxinellu rubra	Gas Plant
Dierama pulcherrimum	Wandflower
Dietes iridiodes	African Iris
Digitalis grandiflorum	Foxglove
Digitalis 'Alba'	Foxglove
Digitalis 'Foxy Miss'	Foxglove
Doronicum caucasium	Leopard's Bane

E

Echinacea purpurea	Coneflower
Echinacea p. 'Shooting Star'	Purple Coneflower
Echinacea p. 'White Luster'	White Coneflower
Epimedium niveum	Bishop's Hat
Epimedium x *versicolor*	Bishop's Hat
Eremurus elwesii	Desert Candle
Erigeron glaucus	Fleabane
Erigeron karvinskianus	Fleabane
Eryngium x *oliverianium*	Sea Holly
Eucomis autumnalis	Pineapple Lily

Euphorbia epithymoides (polychroma)	Cushion Spurge
Euphorbia lophogora	Milkweed; Spurge
Europys mauritanus	False Daisy

F

Filipendula rubra	Queen of the Prairie
Filipendula vulgaris	Meadowsweet

G

Gaillardia x *grandiflora*	Blanketflower
Geranium psilostemon	Cranesbill

Geum quellyon	Avens
Goniolimon tataricum	German Statice
Gypsophila paniculata	Baby's Breath

Opposite: *Baby's breath creeps along the ground and fills the garden with airy clusters of pink or white flowers.* Below: *The bright daises of leopard's bane fill the spring garden, blooming over heart-shaped leaves.*

Broad, handsome clumps of foliage of plantain lily (below) exhibit a
variety of colors, markings, and textures. Opposite left: *Plantain lily brightens the
shade with its yellow-margined leaves, while the daylilies bask in the sun.* Opposite
right: *Hosta is one of the most adaptable perennials in the woodland garden.*

H

Hedychium gardneranum	Kahili Ginger
Helenium autumnale	Sneezeweed
Helianthemum nummularium	Rock Rose
Helianthemum n. 'Fire Dragon'	Rock Rose
Hemerocallis hybrid	Daylily
Hemerocallis 'Johanna'	Daylily
Heuchera sanguinea	Coralbells
Heuchera s. 'June Bride'	Coralbells
Hibiscus moscheutos	Common Rose Mallow
Hosta seiboldii	Seersucker Lily
Hosta venusta	Plantain Lily

I

Iberis sempervirens	Candytuft
Iberis umbellata	Globe Candytuft
Incarvillea delavayi	
Inula ensifolia	Sunray Flower
Iris douglasiana	Pacific Coast Iris
Iris germanica (bearded)	Bearded Iris
Iris kaempferi	Japanese Iris

Iris pseudacorus	Yellow Flag
Iris siberica	Siberian Iris
Iris tectorum	Japanese Roof Iris
Iris xiphium	Spanish Iris

K

Kniphofia uvaria	Red-hot Poker
Kniphofia u. 'Border Ballet'	Red-hot Poker
Kniphofia u. 'Vanilla'	Red-hot Poker

Below: *A border of candytuft surrounds a planting of Iceland poppies in mid-spring.*

Despite its common name, plume poppy is not a true poppy; instead, its flowers appear in fluffy spikes (below).

L

Lamium maculatum	Dead Nettle
Lavandula angustifolia	English Lavender
Leonotis leonurus	Lion's Ear
Leontopodium alpinum	Edelweiss
Liatris spicata	Gay Feather
Liatris s. 'Alba'	Gay Feather
Liatris s. 'kobold'	Gay Feather
Ligularia divorum	Ragwort
Liriope muscari	Lilyturf; Mondo Grass
Lithodora (Lithospermum) diffusa	
Lobelia cardinalis	Cardinal Flower
Lobelia siphilitica	Blue Lobelia

Below: *Money plant is more often grown for the translucent disk that's used in dried arrangements than it is for its rosy purple flowers.*

Lunaria annua	Honesty Plant
Lupinus polyphyllus	Lupine
Lupinus p. 'Russell hybrid'	Lupine
Lupinus hybrid 'Little Lulu'	Lupine
Lychnis coronaria	
Lychnis c. 'Astrosanguinea'	
Lysimachia clethroides	Gooseneck Loosestrife
Lysimachia punctata	Loosestrife

M

Macleaya cordata	Plume Poppy
Malva moschata	Mallow
Monarda didyma	Bee Balm

O

Oenothera missouriensis	Ozark Sundrop
Oenothera speciosa	Evening Primrose
Oenothera speciosa 'berlandier'	Showy Evening Primrose
Oenothera tetragona	Sundrop

P

Paeonia lactifolia	Peony
Paeonia officinalis	Herbaceous Peony
Paeonia suffruticosa	Tree Peony
Papaver orientale	Oriental Poppy
Penstemon g. 'Firebrand'	Penstemon
Penstemon g. 'Huntington Pink'	Penstemon

Opposite: *Popular in China for years, the tree peony is becoming more widely grown in North America for its large, showy flowers.* Below: *Garden peonies bloom in many shades of white, pink, and red, with some as large as dinner plates.*

Penstemon g. 'Miss Leonard'	Penstemon
Penstemon g. 'Ruby King'	Penstemon
Phlox divaricata	Blue Phlox
Phlox paniculata	Border Phlox
Phlox subulata	Moss Pink

Opposite: *Mixed perennials featuring moss pink*. Below: *Sweet William*.

Phormium tenax variegatum	New Zealand Flax
Physostegia virginiana	False Dragonhead
Physostegia v. 'Summer Snow'	False Dragonhead
Platycodon grandiflorum	Balloonflower
Potentilla verna 'aurea'	Cinquefoil
Primula vulgaris	English Primrose
Primula x *polyanthus*	Polyanthus Primrose
Pulmonaria angustifolia	Blue Lungwort
Pyrethrum roseum	Painted Daisy

R

Rehmannia angulata	
Rodgersia aesculifolia	Rodgersflower
Romneya coulteri	Tree Poppy
Rosmarinus officinalis	Rosemary
Rudbeckia fulgida	Black-eyed Susan
Rudbeckia f. 'Goldsturm'	Black-eyed Susan

S

Santolina chamaecyparissus	Lavender Cotton
Satureja montana	Winter Savory
Scabiosa caucasica	Pincushion Flower
Sedum spectabile	Stonecrop
Sidalcea malvaeflora	Checkerbloom
Silene alpestris (quadrifida)	Campion; Catchfly

Like the animal for which it was named, lamb's ear (below) *is soft and furry.*

Silene schafta	Moss Campion
Sisyrinchium bellum	Blue-eyed Grass
Solanum xanthii	
Solidago x *hybrida*	Goldenrod
Stachys byzantina	Betony; Lamb's Ear
Stokesia laevis	Stoke's Aster
Symphytum officinale	

Tiny buttonlike flowers adorn the gray-green, drought-resistant foliage of lavender cotton (below).

Below: *The densely packed, yellow or white spikes of mullein make a bold statement in a sunny border.* Opposite: *Peacock flower.*

T

Teucrium chamaedrys	Germander
Thunbergia battiscombi	Black-eyed Susan Vine
Tigrida pavonia	Peacock Flower
Tricyrtis hirta	Toad Lily
Trollius europaeus	Globeflower

V

Verbascum chaixii	Mullein
Verbena venosa (rigida)	Vervain
Veronica latifolia	
Veronica I. 'Crater Lake'	Speedwell
Veronica I. 'Royal Blue'	Speedwell
Viola cornuta	Tufted Violet

Common—Botanical Name Chart

Common Name	Botanical Name
A	
Alkanet	*Anchusa myosotidiflora*
Allwood's Pink	*Dianthus allwoodii (mixed)*
Aster	*Aster frikartii*
B	
Baby's Breath	*Gypsophila paniculata*
Balloonflower	*Platycodon grandiflorum*
Bear's Breech	*Acanthus mollis*
Bee Balm	*Monarda didyma*
Bellflower	*Campanula glomerata*
Betony	*Stachys byzantina*
Black-eyed Susan	*Rudbeckia fulgida*
Black-eyed Susan Vine	*Thunbergia battiscombi*
Blanketflower	*Gaillardia* x *grandiflora*
Bleeding Heart	*Dicentra spectabilis*

Blood Cranesbill	*Geranium Sanguineum*
Blue-eyed Grass	*Sisyrinchium bellum*
Blue Lobelia	*Lobelia siphilitica*
Blue Lungwort	*Pulmonaria angustifolia*
Bugleweed	*Ajuga reptans*

C

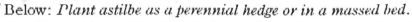

Campion; Catchfly	*Silene alpestris (quadrifida)*

Below: *Plant astilbe as a perennial hedge or in a massed bed.*

Cardinal Flower	*Lobelia cardinalis*
Checkerbloom	*Sidalcea malvaeflora*
Chives	*Allium schoenoprasum*
Climbing Lily	*Clematis 'Nelly Moser'*
Columbine	*Aquilegia a. 'Harebell'*
Columbine	*Aquilegia a. 'Crimson star'*
Columbine	*Aquilegia hybrid*
Common Primrose	*Primula vulgaris*
Coneflower	*Echinacea p. 'White Luster'*
Coralbells	*Heuchera sanguinea*
Cornflower	*Centaurea montana*
Cranesbill	*Geranium cordatum*
Creeping Gypsophila	*Gypsophila repens 'Rosea'*
Cup Sage	*Salvia farinacea*
Cupid's Dart	*Catananche caerulea*
Cushion Spurge	*Euphorbia epithymoides*

D

Daylily	*Hemerocallis hybrid*
Daylily	*Hemerocallis 'Johanna'*
Dead Nettle	*Lamium variegatum*

E

Edelweiss	*Leontopodium alpinum*
Evening Primrose	*Oenothera speciosa*

F

False Daisy	*Europys mauritanus*
False Dragonhead	*Physostegia virginiana*
False Dragonhead	*Physostegia v. 'Summer Snow'*
False Indigo	*Baptisia australis*

Fern-leaved Yarrow	*Achillea filipendula*
Fleabanc	*Erigeron glaucas*
Fleabane	*Erigeron karvinskianus*
Foxglove	*Digitalis purpurea*
Foxglove	*Digitalis p. 'Foxy Miss'*
Foxglove	*Digitalis p. 'Alba'*

G

Garden Pansy	*Viola* x *wittrockiana*
Gas Plant	*Dictamus fraxinella rubra*
Gay Feather	*Liatris spicata*
Gay Feather	*Liatris s. 'Alba'*
Geranium	*Geranium dalmaticum*
German Statice	*Limonium dumosum*
Germander	*Teucrium chamaedrys*
Globeflower	*Trollius europaeus*
Glorybush	*Tibouchina urvilleana*
Goat's Beard	*Astilbe arendsii 'Fanal'*
Goat's Beard	*Astilbe arendsii 'Federsoo'*
Goat's Beard	*Astilbe taquetti 'Superba'*
Goldenrod	*Solidago* x *hybrida*
Golden Star	*Chrysogonum virginiana*
Gooseneck Loosestrife	*Lysimachia clethroides*

H

Heart-leaved Bergenia	*Bergenia cordifolia (white)*
Honesty Plant	*Lunaria annua*

J

Japanese Iris	*Iris kaempferi*

L

Lamb's Ear	*Stachys byzantina*
Lavender	*Lavandula angustifolia*
Lavender Cotton	*Santolina chamaecyparissus*
Leopard's Bane	*Doronicum caucasicum*
Lilyturf	*Liriope musari*
Lion's Ear	*Leonotis leonurus*
Loosestrife	*Lysimachia punctata*
Lupine	*Lupinus polyphyllus (hybrid)*
Lupine	*Lupinus hybrid 'Little Lulu'*

M

Mallow	*Malva maritima*
Masterwort	*Astrantia major*
Meadowrue	*Thalictrum diffusiflorum*
Michaelmas Daisy	*Aster novae-angliae*
Milkweed	*Euphorbia lophogora*
Mondo Grass	*Liriope muscari*
Montebretia	*Crocosmia (montbretia) crocosmiflora*
Montebretia	*Crocosmia (montbretia) masonorum*
Moss Campion	*Silene schafta*
Moss Pink	*Phlox subulata*
Mullein	*Verbascum chaixii*
Mugwort	*Artemesia schmidtiania*

N

New Zealand Flax	*Phormium tenax variegatum*
Nippon Chrysanthemum	*Chrysanthemum nipponicum*

O

Oriental Poppy	*Papaver orientale*
Ozark Sundrop	*Oenothera missouriensis*

P

Pacific Coast Iris	*Iris douglasiana*
Painted Daisy	*Pyrethrum roseum*
Peach-leaved Bellflower	*Campanula persicifolia 'White Star'*
Peacock flower	*Tigrida pavonia*
Penstemon	*Penstemon gloxinoides*
Penstemon	*Penstemon g. 'Huntington Pink'*
Penstemon	*Penstemon g. 'Firebrand'*
Penstemon	*Penstemon g. 'Ruby King'*
Peruvian Lily	*Alstroemaria putchella*
Pincushion	*Scabiosa caucasica*
Pink-flowered Yarrow	*Achillea millefolium roseum*
Pinks	*Dianthus plumarius*
Pineapple Lily	*Eucomis autumnalis*
Plantain Lily	*Hosta alba-margarinata*
Plantain Lily	*Hosta venusta*
Plantain Lily	*Hosta 'Krossa Regal'*

Below left: *Red valerian can add a delightful scent to a bouquet as well as in the garden.* Below right: *Rock rose.*

Purple Coneflower	*Echinacea purpurea 'Shooting Star'*

Q

Queen of the Prairie	*Filipendula rubra*

R

Ragwort	*Ligularia divorum*
Red-hot Poker	*Kniphofia uvaria*
Red-hot Poker	*Kniphofia u. 'Border Ballet'*
Red-hot Poker	*Knifphofia u. 'Vanilla'*
Red Valerian	*Centranthus (Valerian) Ruber*
Rock Rose	*Helianthemum n. 'Fire Dragon'*
Rose Campion	*Lychnis coronaria*
Rosemary	*Rosmarinus officinalis*

S

Savory	*Satureja montana*
Scarlet Sage	*Salvia splendens*
Sea Holly	*Eryngium oliverianium*
Sea Pink	*Armeria maritima*
Self-heal Plant	*Prunella webbiana*

*The bold foliage and showy flowers of ligularia
(ragwort) enable it to stand on its own as an accent plant* (below).

Shasta Daisy	*Chrysanthemum maximum*
Shooting Star	*Cyclamen coum*
Showy Primrose	*Oenothera speciosa 'berlandier'*
Siberian Iris	*Iris siberica*
Silver Mound	*Artemesia schmidtiania*
Sneezeweed	*Achillea ptarmica*
Sneezeweed	*Helenium autumnale*
Snow in Summer	*Cerastium tomentosum*
Spanish Iris	*Iris xiphium*
Speedwell	*Veronica I. 'Crater Lake'*
Speedwell	*Veronica I. 'Royal Blue'*
Spurge	*Euphorbia lophogora*
Stoke's Aster	*Stokesia laevis*
Stonecrop	*Sedum spectabilis*
Summer Border Phlox	*Phlox paniculata*
Sundrop	*Oenothera tetragona*
Sun Rose	*Helianthemum nummularium*
Sweet William	*Dianthus barbatus*
Sweet William	*Phlox divaricata*

T

Threadleaf Coreopsis	*Coreopsis v. 'Moonbeam'*
Thrift	*Armeria maritima*
Toad lily	*Tricyrtis hirta*
Tree Poppy	*Romneya coulteri*

V

Vervain	*Verbena venosa*
Violet	*Viola cornuta*

W

Wandflower	*Dierama pulcherrimum*
White Rockcress	*Arabis albida (caucasica)*
Windflower	*Anemone japonica*
Windflower	*Anemone j. 'September Charm'*
Windflower	*Anemone vitifolia 'Robustissima'*

Y

| Yellow Flag | *Iris pseudacorus* |

Bottom right and left: *Anemone (windflower).*

BEST PERENNIALS FOR SPECIFIC CONDITIONS

Wet Soil Conditions

Arundo 'Donax' (Giant Reed)
Asclepias incarnata (Swamp Milkweed)
Caltha palustris (Marsh Marigold)
Equisetum hyemale (Horsetail)
Gentiana asclepiadea (Willow Gentian)
Helenium (Helen's Flower)
Hibiscus moscheutos
(Swamp Rose Mallow)
Iris pseudacorus (Yellow Flag)
Iris versicolor (Blue Flag)
Lobelia cardinalis (Cardinal Flower)
Lythrum (Loosestrife)
Monarda didyma (Bee Balm)
Myosotis scorpioides
(True Forget-me-not)
Oenothera (Evening Primrose)
Sarracenia purpurea (Pitcher Plant)
Saxifraga (Saxifrage)
Vinca (Periwinkle)

Right: *Bee balm attracts bees and butterflies and can also be used in making tea.*

Dry Soil Conditions

Achillea (Yarrow)
Ajuga reptans (Carpet Bugle)
Anthemis tinctoria
(Golden Marguerite)
Artemisia pycnocephala
Calluna vulgaris (Heather)
Clethra alnifolio (Summer Sweet)
Cornus alba (Tatarian Dogwood)
Cornus stolonifera (Red Osier)
Cornus sanguinea
(Bloodtwig Dogwood)
Hypericum densiflorum
(Dense Hypericum)
Ilex glabra (Inkberry)
Ilex verticillata (Winterberry)
Kalmia angustifolia (Sheep Laurel)
Ligustrum amurense
(Amur Privet)
Pieris floribunda
(Mountain Andromeda)
Rhododendron (Rhododendron)
Sabal minor (Dwarf Palmetto)
Salix (various) (Willow)
Spiraea menziesii (Spiraea)
Spiraea tomentosa (Hardhack)
Vaccinum corymbosum
(Highbush Blueberry)
Viburnum alnifolium (Hobblebush)
Viburnum cassinoides (Withe Rod)
Viburnum dentatum (Arrowwood)

Left: *A variety of low-growing perennials covers the ground between shrubs and bathes it in color. Below right: Mountain rockcress blooms in pink or white and can color the area along pathways in mid-spring.*

Between Paved Areas

Ajuga reptans (Carpet Bugle)
Anthemis nobilis (Chamomile)
Arabis alpina (Mountain Rockcress)
Arenaria montana
Arenaria verna
Armeria maritima (Sea pink or Thrift)
Bellis perennis
Campanula glomerata (Bellflower)
Dianthus (Pink)
Gypsophila repens
Iberis sempervirens (Evergreen Candytuft)
Phlox subulata (Moss Pink)
Sedum acre (Stonecrop)
Sempervivum arachnoideum (Cobweb Houseleek)
Veronica repens (Creeping Speedwell)
Veronica rupestris
Veronica serpyllifolia

Best Ground Cover

Ajuga reptans (Carpet Bugle)
Anthemis nobilis (Chamomile)
Arabis alpina (Mountain Rockcress)
Campanula (Bellflower)
Cerastium tomentosum (Snow-in-summer)
Convallaria majalis (Lily of the Valley)
Drosanthemum floribundum
Gazania splendens (Gazania)
Iberis sempervirens (Evergreen Candytuft)
Lampranthus spectabilis (Trailing Ice Plant)
Malephora croceum (Ice Plant)
Mentha requienii (Mint)
Myosotis (Forget-me-not)
Nepeta mussinii
Pachysandra terminalis (Japanese Pachysandra)
Phlox divaricata (Sweet William)
Phlox subulata (Moss Pink)
Sedum acre (Stonecrop)

Shady Places (Partial Shade)

Acontium anthora (Monkshood)

Ajuga (Bugle)

Althaea rosea (Hollyhock)

Anemonella thalictroides
(Rue Anemone)

Aquilegia hybrids (Columbine)

Asperula (Woodruff)

Campanula rotundifolia (Harebell)

Convallaria majalis (Lily of the valley)

Dicentra spectabilis (Bleeding Heart)

Dictamus albus (Gas Plant)

Epimedium grandiflorum
(Bishop's Hat)

Geranium grandiflorum (Cranesbill)

Helleborus niger (Christmas Rose)

Hemerocallis (Daylily)

Hepatica

Heuchera sanguinea (Coralbells)

Hosta (various) (Plantain Lily)

Hypericum (Saint-Johns-Wort)

Iberis sempervirens
(Evergreen Candytuft)

Lobelia cardinalis (Cardinal Flower)

Mertensia virginica (Virginia Bluebell)

Monarda didyma (Bee Balm)

Phlox divaricata (Sweet William)

Platycodon grandiflorum
(Balloonflower)

Primula (various) (Primrose)

Trollius europeaus (Globeflower)

Although it flowers, hosta is valued for the variety of colors and textures of its foliage that can create a beautiful "all-green" garden in the shade (opposite). Right: *Early spring doesn't seem* complete without an edging of brightly-colored polyanthus primroses. Below right: *Bring a rock wall to life in late spring with an edging of pastel-colored primroses.*

Edging

Woolly achillea tomentosa
(Woolly Yarrow)
Ajuga reptans (Carpet Bugle)
Alyssum saxatile
(Alyssum or Basket of Gold)
Arabis alpina (Mountain Rockcress)
Arabis caucasica (Wall Rockcress)
Armeria maritima (Sea Pink or Thrift)
Aubrietia deltoidea (Rockcress)
Bellis perennis (English Daisy)
Campanula carpatica (Bellflower)
Cerastium tomentosum
(Snow-in-summer)
Dianthus plumarius (Grass Pink)
Festuca ovina 'Glauca' (Blue Fescue)
Heuchera sanguinea (Coralbells)
Iberis sempervirens
(Evergreen Candytuft)
Papaver nudicaule (Iceland Poppy)
Phlox procumbens (Hairy Phlox)
Phlox subulata (Moss Pink)
Primula (Primrose)
Sedum (Stonecrop)
Veronica (Speedwell)
Viola

Near right: *Long-stemmed and fragrant, peonies have had a place in flower arrangements for centuries.* Opposite: *Perennial border.*

Cut Flowers

Achillea (Yarrow)

Anemone japonica

(Japanese Anemone)

Aster

Chrysanthemum morifolium

(Florists' Chrysanthemum)

Delphinium

Dianthus barbatus (Sweet William)

Gaillardia grandiflora (Blanket Flower)

Paeonia (Peony)

City Conditions

Astilbe japonica

Bergenia

Chrysanthemum

Coreopsis

Dianthus barbatus (Sweet William)

Gaillardia

Hemerocallis (Daylily)

Heuchera sanguinea (Coralbells)

Hosta plantaginea (Plantain Lily)

Iris (Bearded Iris)

Paeonia (Peony)

Phlox

Sedum (Stonecrop)

Fragrance

Anthemis nobilis (Chamomile)

Arabis (Rockcress)

Artemisia abrotanum (Southernwood)

Asperula odorata (Sweet Woodruff)

Convallaria majalis (Lily of the Valley)

Dianthus (Pinks)

Dictamus albus (Gas Plant)

Heliotropium arborescens (Heliotrope)

Hesperis matronalis (Sweet Rocket)

Hosta plantaginea (Plaintain Lily)

Lathyrus grandiflorus (Everlasting Pea)

Monarda didyma (Bee Balm)

Oenothera (Evening Primrose)

Paeonia (Peony)

Phlox

Viola odorata (Sweet Violet)

Appendix III

PERENNIALS BY COLOR

WHITE

Achillea ptarmica
(Yarrow)

Althaea rosea
(Hollyhock)

Anemone hypehensis
japonica (Japanese
Anemone)

Anemonella
thalictroides (Rue
Anemone)

Aquilegia (Columbine)

Arabis alpina
(Mountain
Rockcress)

Arabis caucasica (Wall
Rockcress)

Arctotis

Artemisia frigida
(Fringed
Wormwood)

Asperula odorata
(Sweet Woodruff)

Aster

Astilbe

Bellis perennis (English
Daisy)

Bergenia cordiflora
(Heartleaf Bergenia)

Campanula persicifolia
(Peach-leaved
Bellflower)

Cerastium tomentosum
(Snow-in-summer)

Chrysanthemum
coccineum (Painted
Daisy)

Chrysanthemum
maximum (Shasta
Daisy)

Chrysanthemum
morifolium (Florists'
Chrysanthemum)

Convallaris majalis
(Lily of the Valley)

Cornus canadensis
(Bunchberry)

Delphinium hybrid
(Connecticut Yankee
and Pacific Giant)

Deltoides plumarius
(Grass Pink)

Dianthus barbatus
(Sweet William)

Dianthus deltoides
(Maiden Pink)

Dicentra spectabilis
(Bleeding Heart)

Dictamnus albus (Gas
Plant)

Gypsophila paniculata
(Baby's Breath)

Heliotropium
arborescens
(Heliotrope)

Helleborus niger
(Christmas Rose)

Hemerocallis (Daylily)

Hesperis matronalis
(Sweet Rocket)

Heuchera sanguinea
(Coralbells)

Hosta plantaginea
(Plantain Lily)

Iberis sempervirens
(Evergreen
Candytuft)

Iris kaempferi
(Japanese Iris)

Kniphofia uvaria
(Torch Lily)

Lathyrus latifolius
(Perennial Pea)

Limonium latifolium
(Statice, Sea
Lavender)

Monarda didyma (Bee
Balm)

Paeonia (Peony)

Papaver orientale
(Oriental Poppy)

Pelargonium
domesticum (Lady
Washington
Geranium)

Penstemon (Beard
Tongue)

Phlox divaricata (Sweet
William)

Phlox paniculata
(Summer Phlox)

Phlox subulata (Moss
Pink)

Platycodon
  grandiflorum
  (Balloonflower)

Primula malacoides
  (Fairy Primrose)

Polygonatum
  multiflorum
  (Solomon's Seal)

Scabiosa caucasica
  (Pincushion Flower)

Saxifraga (Saxifrage)

Viola cornuta (Tufted
  Viola)

Viola ordorate (Sweet
  Violet)

Yucca filamentosa
  (Adam's Needle)

Below left: *Viola cornuta*. Below right: *Mat-forming moss pink has blue flowers, as well as blooms of white, pink, or lavender.*

BLUE

Anchusa capensis (Summer Forget-me-not)

Aquilegia (Columbine)

Aquilegia alpina (Dwarf Columbine)

Aster frikartii (Aster)

Aster novae-angliae (New England Aster)

Aubrieta deltoidea (Common Aubrieta)

Campanula carpatica (Bellflower)

Campanula rotundifolia (Harebell)

Delphinium hybrid (Connecticut Yankee and Pacific Giant)

Echinops exaltatus (Globe Thistle)

Felicia amelloides (Blue Marguerite)

Gentiana asclepiadea (Willow Gentian)

Heliotropium arborescens (Heliotrope)

Limonium latifolium (Statice, Sea Lavender)

Linum perenne (Blue Flax)

Lithodora diffusa (Gromwell)

Lupinus polyphyllus (Lupine)

Mertensia virginica (Virginia Bluebell)

Myosotis scorpioides (True Forget-me-not)

Penstemon (Beard Tongue)

Phlox divaricata (Sweet William)

Phlox subulata (Moss Pink)

Platycodon grandiflorum (Balloonflower)

Primula malacoides (Fairy Primrose)

Primula polyantha (Polyanthus)

Salvia patens (Blue Salvia or Meadow Sage)

Veronica (Speedwell)

Viola cornuta (Tufted Violet)

Below: *Although blue lupines are effective in a one-colored bed,
they can also be combined with pink, red, yellow, or white varieties.*

LAVENDER

Althaea rosea
(Hollyhock)

Anemone pulsatilla
(Prairie Windflower,
Pasqueflower)

Aquilegia (Columbine)

Aster frikartii (Aster)

Aster novae-angliae
(New England Aster)

Aubrieta deltoidea
(Rockcress)

Bergenia crassifolia

Chrysanthemum
morifolium (Florists'
Chrystanthemum)

Dianthus (Pink)

Digitalis purpurea
(Foxglove)

Hesperis matronalis
(Sweet Rocket)

Hosta plantaginea
(Plantain Lily)

Iris dochotoma (Vesper
Iris)

Paeonia (Peony)

Pelargonium
domesticum (Lady
Washington
Geranium)

Phlox subulata (Moss
Pink)

Primula malacoides
(Fairy Primrose)

Primula polyantha
(polyanthus)

Tulbaghia fragrans

Valeriana officinalis
(Common Valerian)

Vinca minor (Common
Periwinkle)

Viola cornuta (Tufted
Violet)

Below: *Delphinium* x *Belladonna*.

RED

Althaea rosea (Hollyhock)

Anemone hupenhensis japonica (Japanese Anemone)

Aquilegia (Columbine)

Aster

Astilbe (Meadowsweet)

Aubrieta deltoidea (Rockcress)

Digitalis purpurea (Foxglove)

Epimedium grandiflorum (Bishop's Hat)

Gallardia x grandiflora (Blanketflower)

Geranium grandiflorum (Cranesbill)

Hemerocallis (Daylily)

Heuchera sanguinea (Coralbells)

Iris kaempferi (Japanese Iris)

Kniphofia (Red-hot Poker)

Lobelia cardinalis (Cardinal Flower)

Lupinus polyphyllus (Lupine)

Monarda didyma (Bee Balm)

Paeonia (Peony)

Papaver nudicaule (Iceland Poppy)

Papaver orientale (Oriental Poppy)

Pelargonium domesticum (Lady Washington Geranium)

Penstemon (Beard Tongue)

Phlox paniculata (Summer Phlox)

Phlox subulata (Moss Pink)

Primula malacoides (Fairy Primrose)

Primula polyantha (Polyanthus)

Saxifraga (Saxifrage)

Sedum spectabile (Stonecrop)

Senecio (Cineraria)

Viola cornuta (Tufted Violet)

PURPLE-VIOLET

Aquilegia (Columbine)

Aster novae-angliae (New England Aster)

Aubrieta deltoidea (Rockcress)

Chrysanthemum morifolium (Florists' Chrysanthemum)

Dianthus (Pink)

Digitalis purpurea (Foxglove)

Heliotropium arborescens (Heliotrope)

Helleborus niger (Christmas Rose)

Pelargonium domesticum (Lady Washington Geranium)

Platycodon grandiflorum (Balloonflower)

Primula polyantha (Polyanthus)

Viola cornuta (Tufted Violet)

Viola odorata (Sweet Violet)

VIOLET

Anemone pulsatilla
(Prairie Windflower,
Pasqueflower)

Delphinium hybrid
(Connecticut Yankee
and Pacific Giant)

Epimedium
grandiflorum
(Bishop's Hat)

Gentiana ascelpiadea
(Willow Gentian)

Iris kaempferi
(Japanese Iris)

LILAC

Acanthus mollis
(Grecian Urn)

Althaea rosea
(Hollyhock)

PURPLE-LAVENDER

Bergenia crassifolia

Below: *Moss pink*.

PURPLE

Althaea rosea
(Hollyhock)

Armeria maritima (Sea
Pink or Thrift)

Iris kaempferi
(Japanese Iris)

Liatris pycnostacha
(Gay Feather)

Lupinus polyphyllus
(Lupine)

Lythrum (Loosetrife)

Phlox paniculata
(Summer Phlox)

Scabiosa caucasica
(Pincushion Flower)

PINK

Althaea rosea
(Hollyhock)

Anemone hypehensis
japonica (Japanese
Anemone)

Anemonella
thalictroides (Rue
Anemone)

Aquilegia (Columbine)

Armeria maritima (Sea
Pink or Thrift)

Aster

Astilbe (various)
(Meadowsweet)

Aubrieta deltoidea
(Rockcress)

Bellis perennis (English
Daisy)

Campanula carpatica
(Bellflower)

Chrysanthemum
coccineum (Painted
Daisy)

Dianthus barbatus
(Sweet William)

Dianthus deltoides
(Maiden Pink)

Dianthus plumarius
(Grass Pink)

Dicentra spectabilis
(Bleeding Heart)

Digitalis purpurea
(Foxglove)

Heleborus niger
(Christmas Rose)

Hemerocallis (Daylily)

Heuchera sanguinea
(Coralbells)

Iris (Bearded Iris)

Iris kaempferi
(Japanese Iris)

Limonium latifolium
(Statice, Sea
Lavender)

Lupinus polyphyllus
(Lupine)

Monarda didyma (Bee
Balm)

Paeonia (Peony)

Papaver nudicaule
(Iceland Poppy)

Papaver orientale
(Oriental Poppy)

Pelargonium
domesticum (Lady
Washington
Geranium)

Penstemon (Beard
Tongue)

Phlox divaricata (Sweet
William)

Phlox paniculata
(Summer Phlox)

Phlox subulata (Moss
Pink)

Platycodon
grandiflorum
(Balloonflower)

Primula malacoides
(Fairy Primrose)

Primula polyantha
(Polyanthus)

Rudbeckia hirta
(Coneflower)

Saxifraga (Saxifrage)

Sedum spectabile
(Stonecrop)

Senecio (Cineraria)

Tulbaghia fragrans

Veronica (Speedwell)

Viola odorata (Sweet
Violet)

Salmon

Papaver orientale
(Oriental Poppy)

RED-PURPLE

Callirhoe involucrata
(Poppy Mallow)

Lathyrus grandiflorus
(Everlasting Pea)

Lathyrus latifolius
(Perennial Pea)

ORANGE

Althaea rosea
(Hollyhock)

Asclepias incarnata
(Swamp Milkweed)

Asclepias tuberosa
(Butterfly Weed)

Chrysanthemum
morifolium (Florists'
Chrysanthemum)

Dianthus (Pink)

Erysimum asperum
(Siberian
Wallflower)

Gazania hybrids

Geum chiloense
(Coccineum)

Helenium (Helen's
Flower)

Heliopsis (Orange
Sunflower)

Hemerocallis (Daylily)

Kniphofia (Red-hot
Poker)

Linaria vulgaris
(Toadflax)

Papaver nudicaule
(Iceland Poppy)

Papaver orientale
(Oriental Poppy)

Penstemon (Beard
Tongue)

Phlox paniculata
(Summer Phlox)

Primula polyantha
(Polyanthus)

Rudbeckia hirta
(Coneflower)

Strelitzia reginae (Bird
of Paradise)

Viola cornuta (Tufted
Violet)

Iceland poppy (below) *ruffles in the breeze
in shades of orange, yellow, red, white, or pink.*

ROSE

Acanthus mollis
(Grecian Urn)

Althaea rosea
(Hollyhock)

Bellis perennis (English
Daisy)

Bergenia cordifolia
(Heartleaf Bergenia)

Bergenia crassifolia

Dianthus deltoides
(Maiden Pink)

Dianthus plumarius
(Grass Pink)

Dicentra spectabilis
(Bleeding Heart)

Hibiscus moscheutos
(Swamp Rose
Mallow)

Iris kaempferi
(Japanese Iris)

Lysimachia
(Loosestrife)

Phlox paniculata
(Summer Phlox)

Physostegia virginiana
(False Dragonhead)

YELLOW

Achillea tomentosa
(Woolly Yarrow)

Aconitum anthora
(Monkshood)

Althaea rosea
(Hollyhock)

Alyssum saxtile
(Alyssum or Basket
of Gold)

Anthemis nobilis
(Chamomile)

Anthemis tinctoria
(Golden Marguerite)

Aquilegia chrysantha
(Golden Columbine)

Artemisia abrotanum
(Southernwood)

Caltha palustris (Marsh
Marigold)

Centaurea gymnocarpa
(Dusty Miller)

Chrysanthemum
morifolium (Florists'
Chrysanthemum)

Coreopsis grandiflora
(Tickseed)

Dianthus (Pink)

Digitalis purpurea
(Foxglove)

Gaillardia x grandiflora
(Blanketflower)

Gazania hybrids

Geum chiloense
(Coccineum)

Helenium (Helen's
Flower)

Helianthus decapetalus
multiflorus
(Sunflower)

Heliopsis (Orange
Sunflower)

Hemerocallis (Daylily)

Hypericum
(Saint-John's-Wort)

Kniphofia (Red-hot
Poker)

Oenothera (Evening
Primrose)

Paeonia (Peony)

Papaver nudicaule
(Iceland Poppy)

Primula polyantha
(Polyanthus)

Rudbeckia hirta
(Coneflower)

Saxifraga (Saxifrage)

Solidago (various)
(Goldenrod)

Viola cornuta (Tufted
Violet)

Hardiness Zone Map

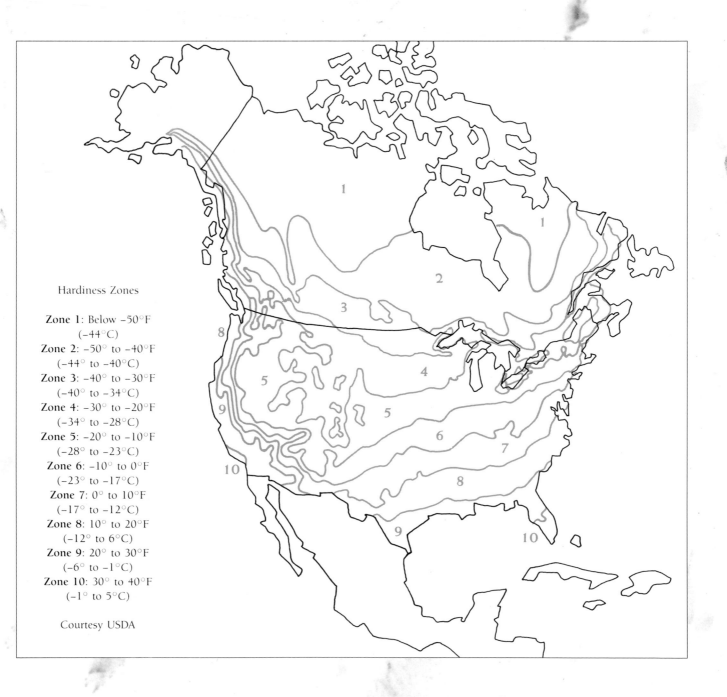

Hardiness Zones

Zone 1: Below –50°F
(–44°C)
Zone 2: –50° to –40°F
(–44° to –40°C)
Zone 3: –40° to –30°F
(–40° to –34°C)
Zone 4: –30° to –20°F
(–34° to –28°C)
Zone 5: –20° to –10°F
(–28° to –23°C)
Zone 6: –10° to 0°F
(–23° to –17°C)
Zone 7: 0° to 10°F
(–17° to –12°C)
Zone 8: 10° to 20°F
(–12° to 6°C)
Zone 9: 20° to 30°F
(–6° to –1°C)
Zone 10: 30° to 40°F
(–1° to 5°C)

Courtesy USDA

Glossary

ALTERNATE Arranged individually along a shoot.

AXIL The angle formed by a leafstalk and the stem.

AXIS The central stalk of a compound leaf.

BASAL LEAF Leaf at base of a stem.

BIENNIAL A plant whose life span extends to two growing seasons.

BRACT A modified and often scalelike leaf.

BUD An undeveloped leaf or flower.

CALYX The sepals of a flower.

CLONE A group of plants originating by vegetative propagation from a single plant.

COMPOUND LEAF A leaf made up of several leaflets.

CORDATE Heart-shaped.

CORM An underground stem.

CORONA A crownlike structure on the corolla of some flowers, such as daffodils and the Milkweed family.

CORYMB A flattened flower cluster.

CREEPER A trailing shoot that takes root at the nodes.

CROWN Part of a plant, usually at soil level.

CULTIVAR A man-made plant variety.

CUTTING A piece of plant without roots.

CYME A branching flower cluster that blooms from the center toward the edges.

DISSECTED A deeply cut leaf.

DIVISION Propagation by division of crowns into segments.

EVERLASTING Flowers for dried arrangements.

FLOWER HEAD A short, tight cluster of flowers.

GENUS A group of closely related species; plural, genera.

GLAUCOUS Covered with a waxy bloom or fine, pale powder.

HIRSUTE Covered with hairs.

HYBRID A plant resulting from a cross between two parent plants belonging to different species.

INFLORESCENCE Flower cluster.

INVASIVE Spreading.

LANCEOLATE Shaped like a spear or lance; narrow at the tip and broadest near the base.

LAYERING Propagation in which a stem sends out roots in surrounding soil.

LEAF AXIL The angle between the petiole of a leaf and the stem attached.

LEAFLET Subdivisions of a compound leaf.

LEAF MARGIN Edge of a leaf.

LOBE A segment of a petal.

MARGIN Edge of a leaf.

MIDRIB The central vein of a leaf or leaflet.

OBOVATE Egg-shaped with broad end at top.

OPPOSITE Arranged along a twig or shoot in pairs, with one on each side.

OVATE Egg-shaped.

PALMATE Having veins or leaflets arranged like the fingers on a hand, arising from a single point.

PANICLE An open flower cluster.

PELTATE A leaf in which stalk is attached to lower surface.

PERENNIAL A plant whose life span extends over several growing seasons.

PETAL One of a series of flower parts.

PETIOLE The stalk of a leaf.

PINNATE A leaf with a series of leaflets.

PROPAGATE To produce new plants, either by vegetative means or by sowing seeds.

RACEME A flower cluster on which individual flowers bloom on small stalks from a larger, central stalk.

RHIZOME A horizontal underground stem.

ROSETTE A circular cluster of leaves; usually basal.

RUNNER A prostrate shoot.

SERRATE Having edges like a saw.

SPATULATE Spoon-shaped.

SPIKE An unbranched inflorescence with stemless flowers.

SUCCULENT A plant with thick, fleshy leaves.

TERMINAL Tip of a stem.

TOOTHED Margin shallowly divided into small, toothlike segments.

TUFTED Growing in dense clumps.

UMBEL A flower cluster.

VARIEGATED Marked, striped.

WHORL Leaves, petals, arranged in a ring shape.

—MAIL-ORDER SUPPLIERS—

The following list of mail-order suppliers is in no way an endorsement for these suppliers. They are companies I have dealt with and found to be satisfactory.

A Selected List of Major Suppliers for Seeds and Catalogs

W. Atlee Burpee Company
300 Park Avenue
Warminster, PA 18974

DeGiorgi Company, Inc.
1409 Third Street
Box 413
Council Bluffs, IA 51502

Farmer Seed & Nursery Company
818 N.W. Fourth Street
Box 129
Fairibault, MN 55021

Henry Field Seed & Nursery Company
407 Sycamore Street
Shenandoah, IA 51602

Gurney Seed and Nursery Company
1224 Page Street
Yankton, SD 57078

Joseph Harris Company, Inc.
3670 Buffalo Road
Rochester, NY 14624

Herbst Brothers Seedsmen, Inc.
1000 N. Main Street
Brewster, NY 10509

J.W. Jung Seed Company
335 S. High Street
Randolph, WI 53957

Liberty Seed Company
128 First Drive SE
Box 806
New Philadelphia, OH 44663

Nichols Garden Nursery
1190 N. Pacific Highway
Albany, OR 97321

L.L. Olds Seed Company
Box 7790
2901 Packers Avenue
Madison, WI 53707

George W. Park Seed Company, Inc.
Box 31
Greenwood, SC 29647

R.H. Shumway Seedsman, Inc.
Box 1
Graniteville, SC 29829

Stokes Seeds, Inc.
737 Main Street
Box 548
Buffalo, NY 14240

Thompson & Morgan, Inc.
Box 1308
Jackson, NJ 08527

Otis Twilley Seed Company, Inc.
Box 65
Trevose, PA 19047

W.J. Unwin Ltd.
Box 9
Farmingdale, NJ 07727

CANADA

Dominion Seed House
115 Guelph Street
Georgetown, Ont.
L7G 4A2